CONSERVATION

edited by
Wendy Pettigrew

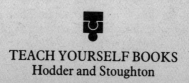

TEACH YOURSELF BOOKS
Hodder and Stoughton

First printed 1982

Illustrations by G. Hartfield Illustrators

Copyright © 1982
Wendy Pettigrew

British Library Cataloguing in Publication Data
Conservation.—(Teach yourself books)
1. Environmental policy—Great Britain
2. Conservation of natural resources—
Great Britain
I. Pettigrew, Wendy
33.7′2′0941   HC260.E5

ISBN 0 340 26821 2

Printed and bound in Great Britain
for Hodder and Stoughton Educational,
a division of Hodder and Stoughton Ltd,
Mill Road, Dunton Green, Sevenoaks, Kent,
by Richard Clay (The Chaucer Press) Ltd, Bungay, Suffolk
Photoset by Rowland Phototypesetting Ltd
Bury St Edmunds, Suffolk

Contents

Acknowledgements

Illustrations
Figs. 2–5 reproduced with permission from Shropshire County Council's *Structure Plan Written Statement 1977*; Figs. 8–11 reproduced with permission from Essex County Council from *Essex Exercise: Farming, Wildlife and Landscape*; Fig. 16 reproduced with permission from *Energy and Transport*, published by Transport 2000, 1974; Fig. 17 reproduced with permission from *Vital Travel Statistics*, published by Transport 2000 and the Open University; Fig. 18 reproduced with permission of the National Society for Clean Air from the journal *Smokeless Air*, No. 155, Autumn 1970; Figs. 19 and 20 reproduced from the Department of the Environment *Digest of Environmental and Water Statistics*, No. 3, 1980. Figs. 23 and 24 reproduced with permission of Friends of the Earth (Birmingham) from *What on Earth are We Doing at Home*; Fig. 25 reproduced with permission of *Vole* and Bryan Reading; Fig. 27 reproduced with permission of the Countryside Commission from *Trends in Tourism and Recreation 1968–78*.

The editor would like to thank all the contributors to this book for their assistance and hard work, and the following people who supplied helpful information and advice: Bernie Sluman, Head of Public Relations, Countryside Commission; David Withrington of the Nature Conservancy Council; Derrick Golland of the National Association for Environmental Education; John Davoll of the Conservation Society; Virginia Blakey of Population Concern; and Bridget Cass of the Council for Environmental Conservation.

List of Figures and Tables

Figures

Tables

Introduction

What is 'conservation'? It can mean different things to different people: to an architect or planner it may mean conserving old and historical buildings; to a museum curator it can mean repairing and preserving historical artifacts; to a naturalist it will mean saving all forms of wildlife from extinction; to the general public it may signify nothing more than recycling used bottles. In fact, these are *all* forms of conservation – which may often mean 'preservation' – of land, plants, buildings, animals. However, conservation is also a way of life: the wise use of all natural resources, weighing up the pros and cons of development and looking to the future needs of society for the basic requirements of everyday life – food, housing, transport, leisure activities and, most important, quality of life in general.

The environment in which we live is a complex one, and everything we do affects it in one way or another. As in an ecological cycle, nothing can be isolated from everything else and deemed to have no effect whatsoever on some aspect of our environment. The same can be said about this book: although the chapters can be read individually, the reader will very quickly realise that they are all interconnected. You can't talk about energy consumption without relating it to transport; you can't discuss forestry without mentioning hill farmers; you can't consider planning proposals without having some idea of what the size of the population will be in twenty or more years' time. It is also important to consider all the different costs and benefits of development and change. Economic considerations are now very important for conservation-minded people, and in many cases it can be shown that conservation pays for itself, and doesn't necessarily cost a lot at all.

The contributors to this book are all people actively involved in conservation, and therefore they are all keen to share their knowledge and experience with those who are just becoming interested in the subject. You may like to know a bit more about them so here is a brief resumé of them all:

Christopher Hall has been Secretary of the Ramblers' Association, Director of the Council for the Protection of Rural England, and is now Editor of the *Countryman*; *Robert Cowan* works for the Town and Country Planning Association as their planning aid officer and is deputy-editor of their journal; *Jim Hall* was a farmer and has recently retired from several years' involvement with the Farming and Wildlife Advisory Group; *George Peterken* is the Nature Conservancy Council's woodland ecologist on their Chief Scientist Team; *Richard Fitter* is the author of many books and field guides on British wildlife and is involved with the Fauna and Flora Preservation Society and their international wildlife issues; *Hugh Miall* is an energy researcher with Earth Resources Research, an independent group linked with Friends of the Earth; *Nick Lester* is Secretary of Transport 2000, a coalition of groups dedicated to environmentally-sound transport planning; *Philip Sharp* is a retired Rear-Admiral who has been involved with clean air issues for many years, notably as Director of the National Society for Clean Air; and *John Corlett* is a marine biologist who has worked for the Ministry of Agriculture, Fisheries and Food and the Natural Environment Research Council; since retiring he has been on CoEnCo's water committee.

That just leaves the editor: I became interested in conservation matters while working in the USA at Princeton University's Office of Population Research. I then moved to California, and spent several years with the Sierra Club (a major US environmental organisation) before returning to Britain where I have been on the staff of the British Trust for Conservation Volunteers, the group which promotes practical conservation work in this country.

The opinions expressed in each chapter are those of the individual authors, and although no effort has been made to present a 'united front', the reader will soon discover that all the contributors agree on basic principles! We all hope that, after reading this book, you will become not only more interested in conservation issues, but also a little more knowledgeable about their complexity, and the problems involved. Each chapter has a short list of books and/or pamphlets which will give you further information, and the list of addresses in Appendix B will be useful for those who would like to become actively involved in conservation matters.

Wendy Pettigrew
Reading, 1981

1 Population

Wendy Pettigrew

Population growth results in increased pressure on all natural resources and threatens the very quality of life which means so much to
us all. More people need more houses, more car owners need more
roads, more food needs to be produced to feed us all, and more TV sets
need to be manufactured to meet consumer demand. As in a pond,
where ripples caused by a small stone hitting the water become larger
and larger and seem like a tidal wave to a small duckling, so even a
small increase in population triggers off many other developments in a
never-ending cycle.

On a global scale, population growth and distribution are of great
concern to both citizens and governments of developed and developing countries. Basic nutrition and housing needs are lowest in countries whose population has overtaken the ability of its own resources to
provide food, shelter and employment. We take for granted our own
high standard of living and would find it hard to imagine what it feels
like to be starving. However, every now and then a little 'crisis' occurs
which makes us realise what life can be like without electricity,
running water and transport. For example, during the drought in the
summer of 1976 many people, particularly in the south-west of
England, were forced to fetch water from stand-pipes in the street.
Yet this is common practice for millions of people in African and
Asian countries. Those of you with an advanced social conscience may
feel this is all unfair – why should we have so much and they so little?
However, there is not a great deal that you, as an individual, can do to
alleviate this situation apart from helping organisations such as
Oxfam, or offering your services to developing countries to help with

medical or educational needs. The efforts of people in developed countries to use their resources wisely will, in the end, benefit people all over the world. Think of yourself first as a world citizen, and secondly as someone living in Britain.

However important the world population problem is to us all, the purpose of this book is to consider conservation matters in Britain, so perhaps it would be best to discuss the pattern of population growth here in recent years, and to think about its likely consequences in the future.

Until about 1750 the birth rate in Britain, as in most of Europe, was high, but so was infant mortality due to malnutrition and primitive medical knowledge. The death rate was also high, often due to wars, epidemics such as cholera, typhus and smallpox, and periodic famines caused by crop failure. From the latter part of the eighteenth century, however, there was a rapid increase in population due to a number of factors. The death rate was reduced by advances in medical knowledge, but this mainly affected the upper and newly-emerging middle classes. The working class life expectancy remained low for some time – it was only 23 years in Liverpool in the 1830s. During the eighteenth century the high alcohol consumption had a devastating effect on mortality rates but this tapered off during the nineteenth century. Increased prosperity meant that people were marrying earlier, and therefore the wife's child-bearing was extended. At the same time, an improved diet with more protein aided this fertility and also extended the lifespan of many people. Even so, food in the new industrial towns was notoriously – and at times lethally – adulterated. An example of this was the use of arsenic to whiten flour! Infant mortality rates were also lowered by the introduction of cotton, a cheap, washable material which greatly improved hygiene standards. The practice of swaddling babies for weeks at a time was no longer necessary. Despite all this, 25 per cent of children died before they were five, but the increased levels of fertility compensated for this, as did the increase in illegitimate births brought about by the breaking up of closely-knit village communities and the move to urban areas.

This reduction in the death rate and increase in births continued throughout most of Western Europe until the early 1900s. Then the spread of contraceptive knowledge, coupled with a decrease in prosperity which delayed marriages in the 1920s and 1930s, caused the birth rate to fall, but the death rate had also fallen so that overall the actual increase in population in some countries was approaching zero by the 1930s. Experts were predicting a downward curve in population growth by perhaps the 1980s – but the increase in births in many countries in the late 1940s (the post-war 'baby boom') and again in the late 1950s and 1960s proved them wrong.

In mid-1979 the population of the United Kingdom was 55.9 million, an increase of 47,000 since mid-1978. This increase was the first since 1974 (when we experienced a reduction in population) and was largely due to the rise in births and a fall in the numbers of people leaving the country. Preliminary results of the April 1981 census show that there are 54.1 million people in England, Wales and Scotland, so the total UK population (when figures for Northern Ireland are available) is likely to have remained fairly static. So how many of us are there likely to be in 2001? Current projections are for a total population of 58.4 million by then, which is interesting when you consider that in 1968 the Registrar General predicted that we would have over 70 million by the turn of the century. The fall in population growth in the UK began in the late 1960s and early 1970s and seems likely to continue, with minor fluctuations, caused by small 'baby booms' such as those occurring after power cuts, television strikes or natural disasters which keep people at home, as well as the rise in births which occurs naturally as the 'baby boom' children reach child-bearing age. This doesn't necessarily mean that the total population in this country will decline (although the Henley Centre for Forecasting has predicted that it could go down to 52 or 53 million by 2000) but that the net increase will be much less and the rate of growth slower.

So why all the fuss about our population growth? If it is already going down, why worry? There are distinct advantages to a population decline in Britain, not the least of which would be an opportunity to show the rest of the world that small can be beautiful, and the many benefits resulting from decreased pressure on our natural resources, the problems of which will be discussed in the following chapters. In the meantime, you, as an individual, can think carefully about your own part in Britain's growth. Will you have children? If so, will your family be limited to two children? If you would like a large family (and can afford it) perhaps you would consider adopting children to raise alongside your own? If you do adopt children, would you consider a child from a deprived background, or of a different race, or perhaps handicapped in some way? This would help ease the burden on our social services and would also help you understand more of other people's problems.

But what has this to do with 'conservation' you ask? Well, it is very difficult to isolate social considerations from environmental ones when studying people. After all, who people live with is as important as where and how they live, as is some knowledge of the age structure of a population so plans can be made for future house building, schools, hospitals and social services. In 1979 the average household in Britain consisted of 2.67 people (not counting dogs and cats), which was a decrease from 3.09 people in 1961. This trend towards smaller 'family' size is expected to continue, not only because of the declining birth rate but also because an increasing number of elderly people live alone. It is anticipated that one-person households in Britain will increase to 6 million by 1991, and over half of these will be of elderly people, although the number of young people living alone is also increasing. But if you have ever looked for a flat or house for one you will know how difficult it is to find something you can afford. Local authorities however are aware of this trend and more 'bachelor' flats are being considered in new housing projects.

Even though 34 per cent of those people aged over sixty-five live alone these days, 51 per cent still live with their spouse, and only 15 per cent live with relatives or in care. As almost 15 per cent of the population is aged sixty-five and over, the care of the elderly in our society is an important factor in organising social welfare. Although most elderly people do prefer to stay in their own home, in familiar surroundings, they often need help – whether with gardening or more essential services such as preparing their meals. They also want to remain as part of the community, leading active and interesting lives. Many who are fit and healthy do a great deal of voluntary work after retirement, and those who are less active welcome the work of younger volunteers and social workers in helping to care for them. If you feel concerned about the place of older people in our society, why not help yourself? Community Service Volunteers, for example, organise young people to help with services for the elderly and infirm, amongst other activities, and your assistance would be most welcome. Or you could 'adopt' elderly neighbours and take the time to help them. Even popping in for a cup of tea and a chat can make a pensioner's day – and you might be surprised what you can learn from talking to older people. You might even consider putting together a series of notes on the history of your town based on information gleaned from conversations with those who have seen changes over the years. Students in the USA have done these as class projects, and have found it a most rewarding and fascinating experience. Your local history society may be interested in helping, so why not contact them?

Another sector of our population needing help and understanding are immigrants to Britain. Migration to and from this country is quite considerable: in 1978-9, 194,000 people left the UK and 187,000 people entered. Since 1971 there has been a reduction in the numbers going to and coming from the old Commonwealth countries (Australia, Canada and New Zealand) while the numbers coming from the 'new' Commonwealth countries have increased as far as the immigration controls will allow, although even these decreased in the early 1980s, no doubt due to the recession in Britain. Immigration of racial minorities results in many social problems, but the fact is that people will continue to want to move to Britain just as some British people will decide that life in Australia is what they have been looking for. Again, the relations between newcomers and the white majority will only be eased by understanding on all sides, and it is most likely that British children going to school with their West Indian or Asian neighbours will get along much better than their parents might have, never having had the opportunity to grow up together. Immigrant families are sometimes larger than others in Britain, but this is often because the young adults who come here tend to have more children than those born in Britain who have moved towards the general pattern of fertility in this country.

For the past 150 years people have been emigrating from Britain to the far corners of the world in search of a better life. However, emigration has its peaks in times of crisis, such as happened in Ireland when the population fell from 8.2 million in 1841 to 6.2 million in 1851 as a result of people dying from or emigrating to escape starvation caused by the potato blight from 1845-8. In more recent years, the energy crises seem to spark off *wanderlust* in some people; in the winter of 1973-4 the High Commissions of Australia and New Zealand were inundated with applications from Britons wanting to move to a place where heating was more readily available, or not needed at all. Unfortunately, even countries with seemingly endless room for newcomers have to control their immigration. Jobs and houses don't grow on trees, even though most of the homes in New Zealand are built of wood! Also, it is very difficult for a family to pack up and move away from relatives, friends – and the local pub. Many do, without knowing any more about the country they are moving to than what they read in books: an immense gamble, and it is not surprising that quite a few return home after a few years. These days, however, young people have much more opportunity to travel and discover the world than their parents did, so any decision they may take to move away is done with much more knowledge of the place they are going to. Still, even with cheap air travel, if you move to Australia you can't expect to come back home every Christmas.

Moving within Britain can also be difficult, and the British are not a race prone to moving from town to town and job to job. If you ever find yourself on a ferry crossing San Francisco Bay, you'll have to talk to at least twenty people before you find someone who was born in the area. Americans are notorious for their rootlessness, finding it easy to move away from home towns. However, they all descend upon the airports at holiday times to return home to family and old friends! Here in Britain, people are much more likely to stay put – Yorkshire-men stay in Yorkshire, Londoners in London. It can also be very difficult to move away from a depressed area to find work elsewhere; no one is around to buy your house and, even if you could sell it, the prices in the boom town will be much higher. You might like to think about your own family – where did it come from, and where are you likely to be in ten or twenty years time? What factors will affect your decision to move, or not? What would happen if thousands of other people did the same as you?

Of course, people have moved in Britain when forced to do so. In 1801, only 16.9 per cent of the population of England were living in urban areas, but this had increased to 53.7 per cent by 1891 as industrial employment offered more money than life as an agricultural labourer. This increase in urban population has continued during the twentieth century, with a marked move to the urban areas of Scotland in the depression years of the 1930s. New advances in agricultural technology have resulted in fewer jobs for farm workers in recent years, and today we are witnessing another technological revolution as computers and the microchip take over and do the jobs of many office and factory workers. This similarly will mean new and different jobs being created for the young, while older people are either made redundant or have to rethink their whole lives and careers. But if supplies of oil do run out, we shall have to consider returning to the land as a greater labour force will be needed to drive the horses and till the soil. Many people are already moving out of the towns, back to the countryside, with dreams of rural self-sufficiency. Whether they make it or not will depend on their own abilities and strength of character to accept an altered lifestyle. Our present demands for material goods, in some cases mainly to impress others, may be our downfall. We need a fast car to get from A to B quickly, but if time was not at such a premium a bicycle would do the job just as well for everyday travel. It won't help a great deal if the population of Britain is reduced or remains relatively static if we continue to increase our consumption of natural resources. It is up to the individual to think carefully about his life-style, and the standard of living to aim for. Always question what you are planning to do, and the effect it will have on other people as well as on the land and its resources. If you live

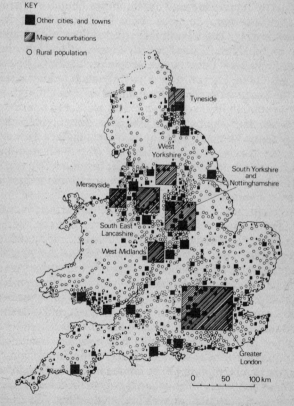

Figure 1   Distribution of population in England and Wales

in a city you may not be too concerned with matters affecting the countryside. Whether the bus service is kept on, or the local factory reduces its air pollution, or your gas bills increase are all likely to seem much more important than the closure of country footpaths or removal of hedgerows. However, we all need the countryside for recreation and food; and our wildlife depends upon it too.

What happens to our towns and cities is also very important, and perhaps this is a good time to think a little about where we live and how many of us live in urban areas. With a population density of 229 people per square kilometre, the UK is one of the most densely populated countries in the world. No wonder we feel there are too many of us! In Europe, Holland has the greatest number of people per square kilometre (412) and, as could be expected, the Japanese manage to cram 313 people into each square kilometre. Compare this to a country like New Zealand, which is approximately the same size as Britain, but has a mere twelve people per square kilometre. No traffic jams there, except after a rugby match, and you can find beaches for solitary sunbathing and forests to walk through without meeting anyone. In Britain you are seldom very far from a settlement, except in the Highlands of Scotland, and cities are crowded with people sometimes literally living on top of one another. However, the least densely populated areas of England (the south-west and East Anglia) are also the fastest growing. Is this because we've used up the space elsewhere? Or perhaps we've got tired of crowds and are longing for wide open spaces and room to breathe.

Even though most of us live in towns, the British have a tradition of longing for a bit of countryside in which to live. Many people dream of retiring to a country cottage (preferably thatched) and lots of us spend our holidays and leisure time in the countryside – camping, hiking, pony-trekking or merely going from village pub to village pub. Again, the increased pressure on recreational facilities in the countryside is causing problems, and is discussed in Chapter 12. Have you ever gone for a walk along a country path, quietly thinking your own thoughts, and been annoyed when you met someone else? They've every right to be there, and probably want to be alone as much as you, but it is ironic that it is difficult to escape from other people for any length of time. Then again, there are lots of people who cannot stand being alone, and life in a crowded town, surrounded by friends and social activities is what they like and would not wish to change. When you are thinking of a career, or generally planning your life, do think about where you want to live. Earning less but living in (for you) the perfect place could be the key to a happy and productive life. Very few of us can have absolutely everything we would like, so decide what you can do without and what you simply must have, and make your choice of lifestyle. Then try to explain it to your family!

Further reading

J Beaujeu-Garnier, *Geography of Population*, Longmans, 1966. This is a standard textbook, but provides a wealth of fascinating information for those who have not studied geography.

Paul Ehrlich, *The End of Affluence*, Ballantine (New York), 1974. An American book which may be hard to find but is worth looking for; in it Ehrlich argues that the time has come for us to question our lifestyle and the effect we are having on consumption of world resources.

Paul Ehrlich and Anne Ehrlich, *Population, Resources, Environment*, Freeman, 1978 (rev.). Standard text on the effect of overpopulation on the world's resources.

Good News about Britain's Population, The Conservation Society, 1980. A four-page pamphlet which shows that Britain will be better off with a decrease in population.

Governmental Statistical Service, *Social Trends 11*, HMSO, 1981. This annual publication provides statistics and analyses them in a way in which everyone can understand.

Deborah Hyams, *World Population Report*, Population Concern, 1979. A twenty-eight-page booklet giving facts and figures about the world's population.

2 Land Use Planning

Christopher Hall

How land is to be used is a community decision. That, broadly, and subject to many imperfections and exceptions, is the unwritten basis of the British planning system. In normal circumstances it is an elected local authority which determines whether the use of a piece of land shall be changed from whatever it now is to something different. Over most of England and Wales the deciding authority is the district council (although decisions about the development of mineral resources are reserved for the county council). In the Greater London area and the metropolitan counties it is the London borough or metropolitan district council which decides, and in Scotland, where the first tier authority is the region, the decision is taken by the district council.

The foundations of planning

The legislative foundation of the British planning system is the Town and Country Planning Act 1947, which established three rules which together form the process known as 'development control':

1   Anyone wishing to change the use of a piece of land, e.g. from farming to housing, or from housing to industry, must first obtain the permission of the local planning authority (see above);
2   The planning authority decides whether to grant or refuse permission against the background of a previously published plan for the area concerned; and
3   The applicant for permission may appeal against its refusal (or

against conditions attached to its grant) to the Secretary of State for the Environment in England, or to the Secretaries of State for Scotland and Wales.

This system has its origins in nineteenth-century attempts to improve public health, and in particular to achieve this by preventing the building of insanitary and unhealthy houses. The first planning Acts (1909 and 1919) began to make it possible for city councils to control the development of housing. Two still relevant features of the system derive from this historic background. First, the anti-slum origins of planning have ensured that planners, who are members of an organised profession subject to common training, are deeply hostile to multiple land use. Official plans almost always show land as zoned for only one type of use (housing, shops, education, agriculture, industry or whatever) unless existing uses are so mixed up that planners see no hope of ever unscrambling them. Thus most planners – though this is less true of the younger generation – have an almost instinctive dislike of what are called in the professional jargon 'non-conforming uses', e.g. a factory in an otherwise residential area. This obviously makes a lot of sense as a means of keeping smoke or chemical pollution or the noise of heavy machinery away from homes, but it puts obstacles in the way of small enterprises which could co-exist harmlessly with houses, e.g. workshops in a village, or a bakery in a town.

The second feature of contemporary planning traceable to its nineteeth-century origins is the building of new towns and garden cities. The key historical figure in this was Sir Ebenezer Howard (1850–1928) the founder of the garden city movement, which aimed to combine the conveniences of urban living with the health and recreational benefits of a rural life. With the population of the older conurbations static or declining, and with the growing belief that old city centres should be revitalised, the new town ethos has declined in importance, but evidence of its compelling idealism remains in the pioneering model suburbs built by industrialists, e.g. Port Sunlight (1887) and Bourneville (1878), in the garden cities of Letchworth (1907) and Welwyn (1920), and in the post-war new towns, the last generation of which were planned in the 1960s and are still growing, e.g. Milton Keynes (1967), Telford (1963) and Warrington (1968). One of the principal pressure groups seeking to influence government planning policy is the Town and Country Planning Association

(TCPA), originally founded as the Garden Cities Association. Today its main role is to argue against high density housing – especially large blocks of flats – in favour of individual houses and gardens dispersed through what it calls 'city regions'. Two-storey houses with small gardens need take up no more total space than the same amount of built living space arranged in high-rises. Whether this is a sensible use of limited and dwindling agricultural land in a small country is a basic conflict in planning today, the more difficult to resolve because people on both sides of the argument invoke conservationist principles.

The TCPA point to the failures of post-war city planning in which the options were either up or out – up into soul-less high-rise tower blocks or out into faceless housing estates on the urban fringe. Those who do not go all the way with the TCPA belong to the anti-urban tradition of British planning and conservation, a movement which has had and still has a powerful political impact. Conservationists in this tradition reacted to industrial slum cities and the sprawling ribbon development of the inter-war period by giving first priority to the preservation of the countryside.

'God made the country, and man made the town,' wrote the poet William Cowper in the middle of the Industrial Revolution. And at more or less the same time, William Wordsworth and the Lake poets were discovering the long-despised virtues of wilderness and inveighing against the spread of railways which might endanger their paradise with more people and development. The chief pressure groups in this tradition are the Council for the Protection of Rural England (CPRE) (1926) and the Ramblers' Association (1935). The CPRE has equivalent groups in Scotland and Wales.

Much of the legislation to protect the countryside stems from the efforts of bodies like these. Their long-term success – despite the fact that some 30,352 hectares of countryside are currently estimated to be lost to other uses each year – is evidenced by the fact that, of the 151,000 square kilometres of England and Wales, about 75 per cent remain under farming or forestry. Although both past and present statistics are imprecise, it is certain that this proportion is only a few percentage points different from what it was in 1920 when the population was only 37 million compared with 48.5 million fifty years later. The figures are even more striking if Scotland with its very much higher proportion of agricultural and afforested land is included.

The Town and Country Planning Act 1947 crowned the campaign

by preservationists (the term 'conservationist' was not then in use) to restrain and control urban expansion, but the period 1944–55 also saw the launching of a series of other statutory controls and government initiatives which complemented that Act and which constitute the framework within which conservationists work today. The main measures were:

The Town and Country Planning Act 1944. This Act began the process of listing buildings 'of special architectural and historic interest'. Listing is now the responsibility of specially trained investigators in the Ancient Monuments and Historic Buildings Directorate of the Department of the Environment (DOE). By 1981 a total of about 250,000 buildings had been listed. Such buildings may not be altered or demolished without 'listed building consent' granted by the local planning authority. However, a determined owner, who can see big profits in redeveloping a site occupied by a listed building, may well prefer to pay the fine for demolishing the listed building rather than search for another site. Applications for consent have to be advertised and must be notified to certain national architectural conservation societies. A threatened building not already protected may be 'spot listed' as an emergency measure by the DOE as a result of information received from a local authority, society or individual. Although the total of listed buildings sounds impressive, conservationists believe that as many as 700–800,000 should be listed, and that the DOE staff available for the task of completing and updating the lists is quite insufficient.

The National Parks and Access to the Countryside Act 1949 provided for the establishment of national parks and areas of outstanding natural beauty to protect especially beautiful areas of countryside in England and Wales. (For details of these designations and the different position in Scotland see below, and for the Act's recreational provisions see Chapter 12.) The Act also laid the groundwork for another aspect of conservation, the protection of wildlife, through the setting up of what is now the Nature Conservancy Council (a government agency) with powers to create national nature reserves and to designate sites of special scientific interest (SSSIs).

Green Belts, Circular No 42/55, Ministry of Housing and Local Government. This was not an Act of Parliament, but in effect a directive by the ministry then responsible, calling on local planning authorities to establish 'green belts' of undeveloped land in order to prevent urban sprawl, check the merging of communities and protect the character of historic settlements.

This completed the planning system in roughly the shape it is still in today. Essentially it is in two parts: 1) a laid-down procedure for settling the use of individual pieces of land, and 2) a background of national and local planning policies and designations governing these decisions. In both – and we now look at them in more detail – there are ample opportunities for conservationists to express their views and exert influence on the land use planning of their localities and of the country as a whole.

The planning decision

Suppose that Mr Bloggs, a house builder, wishes to develop an estate of private houses on land on the edge of the town of Blankville. At present the land is farmed. What are the steps which Mr Bloggs must take to get permission for his new estate, and what chances do those who oppose such a plan have to influence the outcome?

His first consideration will be whether an application for change of use has enough chance of success to make the trouble of an application worthwhile. If the land is zoned as green belt and if the Blankville District Council is known for its rigorous preservation of its green belt he is unlikely to make an application, unless (as may well be the case) he knows the government favours releasing more protected land in that area for housing. If so, he may think that, although the Council will refuse permission, his chances of winning ministerial approval on appeal are good.

Having decided to make an application he does so on a standard form provided by the Council. He can either seek 'outline permission' or 'detailed permission'. The phrases are more or less self-explanatory. Outline permission might give approval for the building of not more than X number of houses on the land, subject to later approval of 'detailed' design and layout. The Council however will have to pay substantial compensation to Mr Bloggs if, having granted outline planning permission and thus immensely increased the value of his land above its agricultural value, they later fail to give him detailed permission, so rendering the land unusable except for farming.

On receipt of the application the Council has a number of administrative steps to take, such as informing bodies called 'statutory undertakers' (e.g. the electricity board and the regional water authority) so that they can comment on the proposal. They also have to inform the Local Council (if any) which has the right to make its views known to the District Council. (Local Councils are Parish Councils in England and Community Councils in Wales, plus those former urban districts and boroughs which lost that status on the re-organisation of local government in 1974. In particular, the District Council must enter the application on the public planning register.)

It would be impossible in the space available to describe all the various courses which Mr Bloggs' application might now take. Many minor and straightforward applications (e.g. plans to extend a house by the addition of a new room) are in fact taken by council officers acting under powers delegated to them by the elected councillors, in which case there is relatively little opportunity, other than by a letter to the Council's planning officer, for public influence on the decision. But Mr Bloggs is interested, let us suppose, in a sizeable number of acres. There is public concern about his proposal, and perhaps doubts on the part of the regional water authority about whether the existing sewerage system can cope with the proposed new estate. So the issue must be decided by councillors and specifically by the Council's planning committee.

Before that committee meets – and Mr Bloggs is entitled to have his answer within two months of his application – those who object to the proposal or wish to have it modified (e.g. by reducing the number of houses on the land or by insisting on the retention of certain trees) can campaign against it. Such a campaign will concentrate on those councillors serving on the planning committee and those elected to represent the parts of the district most affected by the scheme. If the application falls within the territory of a local council, its members can also be approached to seek their support and to express it to the District Council.

The planning committee has three options: to grant permission, to refuse permission, or to grant permission subject to conditions. If they take the first option that is almost certainly the end of the matter. No challenge to the Council's decision is possible except on the grounds that they have failed to comply with the law – and the law does not dictate what is a right or wrong planning decision. But if Mr Bloggs' application is refused, or if it is granted subject to conditions which he dislikes, then *he* may appeal to the Secretary of State against the Council's decision.

Such an appeal may be settled by written representations, i.e. the appellant, the Council and its supporters argue the matter out in a paper debate conducted by civil servants, who eventually recommend a decision to the Secretary. But in controversial cases an appeal will usually be dealt with by public inquiry, a procedure which provides the concerned conservationist with a great deal of scope for influencing the final ministerial decision.

The public inquiry

Here the procedure is a mixture of a public meeting and a court of law. The theory is that the Inspector (called a Reporter in Scotland) appointed by the Secretary of State chairs the proceedings, listens to all the evidence and then prepares a report with a recommendation to the Secretary of State, who may or may not accept the recommendation. The inquiry is supposed to be informal and it is certainly true that the Inspector will ensure that any individual can have his say. But public inquiries have been steadily taken over by lawyers. In the hypothetical appeal by Mr Bloggs, the Council's case will almost certainly be put by a member of their legal staff (a solicitor) and if Mr Bloggs chooses to employ a barrister then probably the Council will too. (In big set-piece inquiries raising issues of national importance scores of barristers may attend.)

At an inquiry you can stand up, state your opinion off the top of your head and sit down. You will be heard in silence but what you say won't carry much weight. A better approach is to write down what you want to say (you'll say it better for having thought it out carefully beforehand anyway); and make plenty of copies. The inspector and the other side will want one, and if you hand them to the local newspaper reporters you may get some publicity into the bargain. Your written statement is called a 'proof of evidence' and you should read it slowly (very few inspectors have shorthand). After that you are subject – as in a law court – to cross-questioning by the other side.

When the inquiry is over the Inspector prepares his report for the Minister who then decides the matter. There is no appeal other than on questions of whether the law has been properly observed.

Increasingly, the role of public inquiries is coming under critical scrutiny. For minor and local issues it is generally accepted that they serve their purpose well enough. The opinions expressed are fairly conveyed to the Secretary of State who, having no special interest one way or the other in the matter, is able to make a decision which, if not agreeable to all, is at least accepted as a fair judgment. But it is more questionable whether an inquiry in which the Minister makes the final decision is the appropriate way of dealing with proposals *which themselves form part of government policy.*

For instance, the present government is committed to a policy of expanding nuclear power in Britain. It seems, to say the least, unlikely that objectors to the building of nuclear power station proposals will accept the Environment Secretary, himself a Cabinet minister, as a neutral arbitrator. The fact that public inquiries are not in theory supposed to be courts of law in which the Minister plays the judge's role will not alter that feeling. Ministers and the public alike have increasingly come to treat them as debating platforms in which all points of view can be freely expressed, and it is contrary to a sense of natural justice that thereafter the matter should be decided by an interested party who has himself helped formulate the policy which has given rise to the inquiry.

The same dilemma arose at inquiries into new roads proposed as part of the government's motorway and trunk road programme in the mid 1970s, when objectors began to question the road construction policy as such. Eventually the government felt compelled to restrict the scope of these inquiries; and in a celebrated case – that of the M42, Warwick to Umberslade section – the House of Lords ruled that objectors had no right to cross-examine Department of Transport witnesses on the policy behind a particular road scheme. As the nuclear power programme develops, this ruling will presumably be used to prevent challenges to the overall nuclear energy policy – no doubt with lively results. Some conservationists believe that the inquiry system will break down under the pressure of civil disobedience which they expect objectors to employ, and that, as a consequence, government will either abandon the programme or adopt more draconian means of pushing it through with the minimum of public participation.

Plans, designations and exceptions

Public inquiries are the most dramatic and newsworthy part of the planning process, but the vast majority of planning applications never get anywhere near a public inquiry, either because the decision is so straightforward and uncontroversial that an aggrieved developer never considers appealing against it; or because the objectors to the application have no right of appeal anyway. In addition, a great many changes of land use are deemed not to require planning permission at all. Any conservationist concerned with his local environment needs to be familiar with the General Development Order. This is not an Act of Parliament, but a statutory instrument which automatically grants planning permission to certain developments. The main categories of such development are small household extensions, agricultural works and buildings, and forestry.

From the conservationist's point of view these exceptions to the system are all more or less deplorable. While many minor household developments are innocuous, in a street-scene of homogenous buildings one ill-considered addition can jar. The exceptions for agriculture and forestry are in no way justifiable. Both industries have major impacts on the landscape and on wildlife and recreation. A hedgerow rich in wildlife that has stood for 500 years or more can be destroyed in half a morning by a bulldozer, while a listed building of far less antiquity and interest may be subject to a sophisticated system of protection. A forest of conifers can engulf a moor or mountainside without any public consultation and without the community nationally or locally having any say in the matter.

Only the bigger farm buildings (floor area greater than 465 square metres, or more than 12 metres high) and those close to roads are subject to planning control, except in some areas of our National Parks, subject to Landscape Areas Special Development Orders. But *any* kind of development normally exempted from the system may be brought within it by means of the rarely used Article IV direction procedure, under which the planning authority withholds deemed consent. Such orders are subject to ministerial approval.

In reaching any planning decision the planning authority must take account of relevant statutory plans or designations. These are of two kinds: designations made nationally; and plans or designations made by local authorities. There are four major designations; three of which cover sizeable areas of countryside:

National Parks: There are ten (listed in Chapter 12, p. 159) which cover about 10 per cent of England and Wales. (Scotland has no national parks, mainly because the powerful landowning interest opposed a designation which they feared might hamper their freedom.) They are designated by the Countryside Commission (formerly the National Parks Commission), a government agency, after consultation with the public and local authorities. Their purpose is to preserve and enhance the natural beauty of the landscape and to provide appropriate recreation. Where these two aims conflict, it is government policy to give priority to conservation. Since there is no practical prospect at this time (1981) of further parks being designated, the conservationist's opportunity is limited to seeking to prevent their misuse. Remember that national park status does not imply public ownership. Planning permissions can still be sought by individual owners and developers in the same way as anywhere else, although the park authorities (boards or committees consisting mostly of county councillors, but with one-third of the members appointed by the Secretary of State) do generally exercise rigorous development control policies. The parks are also vulnerable to developments especially suited to their soils e.g. mineral extraction and afforestation. Minerals are generally found beneath the geologically older rocks which form the more dramatic landscapes. The forestry industry usually buys the less expensive marginal moorlands – again a special feature of park scenery – for planting.

The national park authorities are required to prepare and maintain management plans for the conservation and enjoyment of their areas. Extensive public participation is invited.

Areas of Outstanding Natural Beauty (AONBs): A further tenth of England and Wales is covered by this unwieldy and bureaucratic sounding designation (see Chapter 12 for a list of the areas). AONBs originated as particularly beautiful areas which it was considered impracticable to designate as national parks. Their statutory objective is the same as that for the parks, but there is no requirement to provide for recreation. Their administration remains in the hands of local planning authorities, and is in no way different from any undesignated area. Generally, development control policies are somewhat tighter inside AONBs than out, but this is not always the case. Since these are mostly more inhabited than the national parks, a good deal of development that conflicts with the beauty of the countryside may occur. Conservationists, however, find the designation a useful card to play in fighting undesirable developments.

Both national parks and AONBs exist to protect fine landscapes. The next two designations – though they may also serve that purpose – have other objectives.

Green Belts: In these, the aims of designation (by the local authority subject to approval by central government) are as set out on page 13. Thus most green belts, since they comprise the fringe of large towns, necessarily incorporate countryside which is less than beautiful, for example areas of run-down farming where horses are the main crop, and odd corners of field and copse, stuck between sewage farms and golf courses and bisected by main roads.

In general, local authorities run very tight development control policies for the belts, perhaps because this is the one planning designation which, though often misunderstood, has become part of the common language, and which commands genuine public support. But certain non-rural uses are traditionally allowed in the belts, e.g. golf courses and educational institutions.

There are green belts round most of the major English conurbations, the Metropolitan Green Belt around London being the first and most famous. Government policy is to keep the belts narrow, perhaps as little as five to eight kilometres deep, on the grounds that a wider designation cannot be sustained against pressure for development.

Sites of Special Scientific Interest (SSSIS): There are 3800 of these throughout Britain, designated by the Nature Conservancy Council. Their title and purpose is self-explanatory: they are places where particularly important plant or wildlife species or communities exist. SSSIs enjoy little protection other than official recognition. They are not publicly owned and many of them are damaged every year, usually by agricultural operations: e.g. the draining of wetlands or the removal of cover vegetation. By the Wildlife and Countryside Act 1981 owners and occupiers of SSSIs are required to give notice of intention to undertake any operation which may damage the site, but no power exists to prevent this damage actually being done except by a voluntary code of practice which is being drawn up at the time of going to press. In a few selected sites the Nature Conservancy Council will have power to delay damaging operations for up to one year while seeking to make a management agreement with the owner or occupier.

Another designation of wildlife significance, though it is imposed primarily for amenity purposes, is the *Tree Preservation Order* (TPO). This forbids the felling of the tree or trees concerned and is instituted by the local authority. TPOs are frequently made as a result of threats to standing timber being drawn to the authority's attention by members of the public or local environmental groups.

Structure and local plans: These are types of plans, with the various designations included within them, and are made locally. The structure plan is prepared for each county and is now the only major planning function left at county council level. The structure plan is in fact a series of volumes covering every aspect of the physical planning of the area – transport; which towns and villages are to be expanded and which restricted; education; shopping and health provisions; and where they are located. This is planning in the very widest sense. Structure plans do not attempt to settle the exact future use of every piece of land, instead they aim to set a broad, flexible picture within which the development control authorities (district councils) can operate.

Elaborate consultation procedures are laid down culminating in the plan's 'examination-in-public'. This is a kind of extended public inquiry under a chairman nominated by the Secretary of State. It looks at particular topics in the plan and discusses them with representatives of the county council, other local authorities, statutory agencies, such as water authorities and tourist boards, and local societies and individuals. To the alert

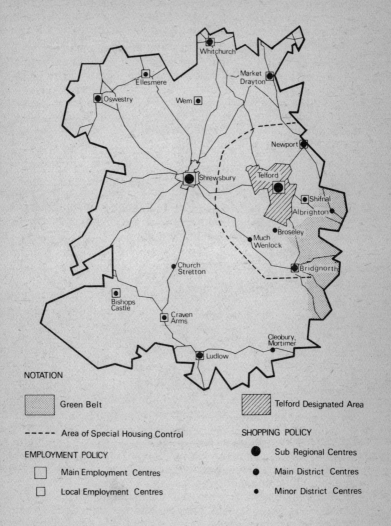

Figure 2   Settlement structure in Shropshire

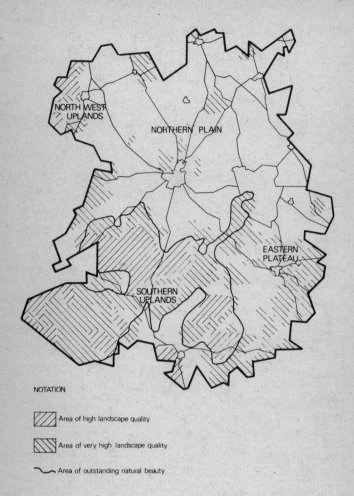

Figure 3 Landscape quality in Shropshire

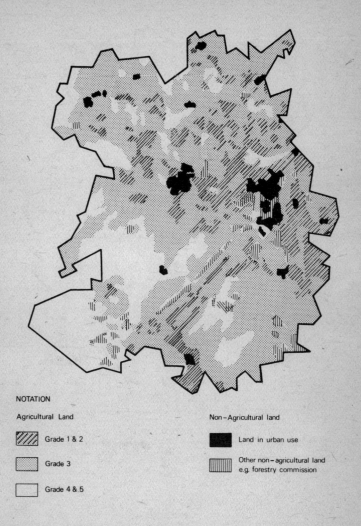

NOTATION

Agricultural Land   Non-Agricultural land

Grade 1 & 2   Land in urban use

Grade 3   Other non-agricultural land
                                                    e.g. forestry commission

Grade 4 & 5

Figure 4   Agricultural land quality in Shropshire

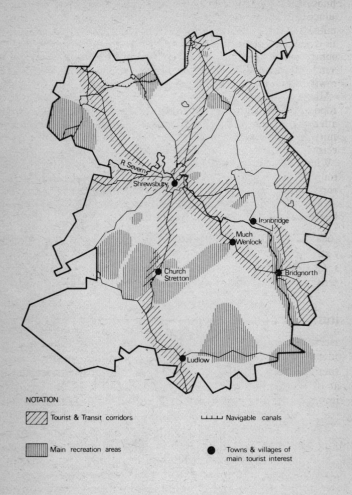

Figure 5   Recreation and tourism in Shropshire

conservationist the examination-in-public offers the chance to probe the philosophical and political bases of official policies. For instance, a county council settlement policy whereby new council houses in rural areas are limited to a few growth villages might be challenged on the grounds that this is making it impossible for the smaller communities to survive. Or, the county council could be pressed to attach special landscape value to a stretch of countryside threatened with development or to restrict the growth of a town threatened with over-population.

After examination, the plan goes to the Secretary of State, who usually proposes modifications in the light of government policy and conformity with adjacent plans. These are published in draft giving a further opportunity for public comment. The Secretary of State then makes his final decision and approves the plan as amended.

Within the framework of the structure plan the county council or groupings of county and district councils make local plans – detailed proposals for particular areas or for the handling of particular problems – e.g. a county might have a plan for its mineral resources. Plans are open to objection and public inquiry on matters of detail.

Local authorities also designate conservation areas in which specially strict controls are applied for the preservation of historic buildings. Consultative committees linking the local authority with local citizens' groups have been set up for many such areas.

Criteria for conservation

Conservation is at best a very vague word. A typical definition is: 'Modern conservation is a dynamic, evolving concept of co-partnership between man and nature. It requires the strict management of each resource – land, air, water and wildlife – to ensure optimum value and continuity of supply.'* As a definition, this is pretty useless: whose is the 'optimum value'?

Consider a Department of Transport proposal to build a by-pass round an historic town. The Department will argue that by so doing they will conserve the town's old buildings, now being shaken by juggernauts, and return peace and quiet to the High Street, thus greatly improving the quality of life there. Objectors will argue that the by-pass will take needed farmland, destroy habitats for wildlife and disrupt footpaths used for recreation. A similar conflict of conservationist arguments occurs in relation to almost every major

* From *Man and Environment*, Robert Ardill, Pelican Original, 1967, p. 170.

development. Even nuclear energy, condemned by most active conservationists, can be supported with respectable arguments, e.g. that it is pollution-free and that it obviates the need to use up finite resources, such as coal.

Sometimes these conflicts depend on where you live. The resident in the High Street will be a different sort of conservationist from the farmer in the fields where the by-pass will run. More importantly they depend on whether you are a micro- or macro-conservationist. The question the individual has to settle is how far to go. The macro-conservationist solution to the traffic problem is to reconstruct the economy into small units of production selling direct to local markets and therefore not needing long distance transport. The micro-solution is to push a bit more traffic on to rail and build by-passes as well-designed and landscaped as possible.

A good way of deciding which kind of conservationist you are is to try to use the opportunities for pressure and change in the planning system which this chapter has described. Most of these opportunities are geared to micro-conservation. If you find that from doing this you get rewarding results which satisfy you, then you are a micro-conservationist. On the other hand, if you yearn for a more revolutionary approach – even at the cost of less effective achievement – you are macro-.

Further reading

Paul Cloke, *Key Settlement in Rural Areas*, Methuen, 1979. (A critique of the rural planning orthodoxy of the post-war period.)

Department of the Environment and Welsh Office, *Report of the National Parks Policy Review Committee*, HMSO, 1974. (Known as the 'Sandford Report', this is the only major official review of the National Parks system since its inception.)

Andrew W Gilg, *Countryside Planning*, David & Charles, 1978. (A useful summary of the period 1945–76.)

Bryn Green, *Countryside Conservation*, George Allen and Unwin, 1981. (A useful review of the main issues.)

Ann and Malcolm MacEwen, *National Parks: Conservation or Cosmetics?*, George Allen and Unwin, 1981. (The most searching and challenging study yet of the parks system.)

Marion Shoard, *The Theft of the Countryside*, Temple Smith, 1980. (A famous attack on the agricultural industry's destruction of landscape which emphasises the lack of planning control over farming and forestry.)

Clough Williams-Ellis, *England and the Octopus*, Antonine Publishing Co, 1975. (A new edition with an introduction by Lewis Mumford; a classic written in 1928 when landscape protection first became a national concern.)

The Town and Country Planning Association's Planning Aid Unit publishes several leaflets which may be helpful: *How to make representations on an application for planning permission*; *Protecting trees – a guide to legislation*; *Your right to attend planning committee meetings*; and *Conservation areas*. (All 25p at time of going to press.) They also publish a weekly *Planning Bulletin* and monthly newsletter, *Planning Aid*.

3 Urban Development

Robert Cowan

Urban areas are constantly changing. New houses are built, old streets are demolished, declining areas suddenly become fashionable and are rehabilitated by their new owners, odd pieces of wasteland appear, a housing estate begins to get a bad name, and so on. There are people whose job it is to try to plan and control how our towns and cities develop, but they find it difficult. In many ways it is a mystery why a particular place develops as it does, and there is no certain way of guiding the future. Even when planners think they know what they want to do, they often find that they do not have the means to do it.

There is great concern nowadays that the inner-city areas are dying and becoming derelict. Their decline might be explained as a physical symptom of society adapting to new circumstances: but that is of little comfort to the people – often the old and poor – who find their surroundings going downhill. Living with urban change can be painful.

But that is nothing new. The growth of Britain's great cities at the beginning of the nineteenth century was much faster than their decline now. People flocked into them to find work in the new factories, and many were housed in unhealthy, overcrowded slums which were built at the same time. It was the belief among some social reformers that change need not lead to such intolerable human misery that inspired the town planning movement in Britain at the beginning of this century.

In 1898 Ebenezer Howard published the book that he later titled *Garden Cities of Tomorrow*. In it he outlined what he thought were practical proposals for how everyone would eventually be able to live in pleasant surroundings, as a result of rational planning. He hoped to persuade people that building garden cities would solve the urban problems – and the associated problem of rural depopulation – that were the legacy of the Victorian age. Howard proposed that proto-types should be built to demonstrate the idea, and that garden cities should then be built throughout the country. He managed to recruit enthusiastic supporters and eventually two garden cities were built – at Letchworth and Welwyn in Hertfordshire. They were small indus-trial towns which showed the essential features of the garden city idea: they were carefully planned and their development was closely con-trolled; their size was limited, and they were surrounded by a belt of agricultural land; and the land on which the garden cities stood was owned by their corporations, which leased the land back for housing, industry and other purposes. This last feature meant that when the value of the land rose as the green fields became a town, the increase became an asset of the community itself rather than of speculators or commercial developers.

The garden city movement was successful in gaining support for the idea of town planning, but was neither powerful nor influential enough to redirect the flood of *unplanned* development between the two world wars into a programme of garden city building. No more than the two garden cities were ever built, and the restructuring of Britain's urban areas – which Howard had claimed would be the inevitable result of a major garden city programme – did not happen; or at least, not in the way that the garden city pioneers had planned.

This century has seen dramatic changes in the patterns of urban development. As car ownership increased, and as new railway lines were built to carry commuters to the city centres, large monotonous suburbs were built and new development sprawled along main roads and across the countryside. Although laws were passed to prevent such unplanned development, what did eventually stop it was not legislation, but the Second World War; for not only did the war bring a pause in urban development, it also gave the nation a taste of what could be achieved by planning and co-ordination on a large scale.

The national will that helped win the war, it was argued, must be used to rebuild Britain. A comprehensive system of town planning was created, and a programme of building new towns was launched. The new towns were not what the garden city pioneers had hoped for – the increase in the value of their land did not become an asset to be used for the benefit of the community, for example – but the programme was a bold attempt at creating new communities by rational planning. Between 1946 and the late 1960s, thirty new towns were built, and now have a total population of over 2 million.

The new towns are considered to be a success. They have succeeded in attracting industrial development offering employment and have shown that a living, working town can be built from scratch. Overseas visitors come to marvel at these wonders of British planning. But some people have their doubts. The new towns seem to have everything going for them: a development corporation for each town with the power to get things done, the best architects and planners, and enough money to do the job. So why do they still have social problems? Sociologists delight in showing us that the new towns have similar problems to the old, and others have described the new towns as soul-less. It depends on what you compare them with. What should a town offer – the elegance of Bath, the character of York, the vitality of Leicester Square, the tranquility of Ambridge, or the sociability of Coronation Street? After the bold claims of the new towns movement, people had high expectations. But the popular image of what makes a good place in theory will often be beyond the scope of what planners can provide in practice. The new town builders have had to erect large numbers of houses, in a short time and at a low cost, for people who do the same sort of jobs and live the same sort of lives as people elsewhere. Some of the results have been very good, others have not.

Compared with other post-war urban development in Britain, the new towns show up well. They account for only a small proportion of the development: the rest have included large estates of council housing, sprawling suburbs, and additions to existing towns and villages of all sizes. Some places are threatened with being swamped by new development, and their residents have campaigned to halt this and to conserve the character of the environment. Of the council estates, some house as many people as a new town, but lack the facilities and nearby employment. When they were built, the urgent need to put up houses to replace the slums meant that there was little political support in some places for building anything on the estates other than houses. Nowadays there are complaints that there is more to satisfactory living conditions than having a decent house, and some people look back fondly to the slums they left, remembering the corner shops, the friendly neighbours and the sense of community. But a living community does not only flourish in a slum area, and nostalgia sometimes dulls the memory of how bad the houses were.

Figure 6 High-rise flats – the planner's dream, or nightmare? (*Robert Cowan*)

A lot of post-war council housing was in the form of high flats, of anything from six to thirty storeys. As a result, in Great Britain in 1977 nearly a quarter of a million children aged up to fifteen were living in flats above the first floor; but the General Household Survey (Office of Population Censuses and Surveys, 1979) on which that figure was based found in its sample not one child of professional parents who lived above the first floor! While the imaginations of the architects and the planners soared, they and their own families remained firmly on the ground. It is now generally agreed that the widespread construction of high-rise housing was a mistake, as the expensive practice of building high brought no benefits. The fault was not that of the architects and planners alone; local politicians believed that high-rise housing would be a means of maintaining the populations of the inner areas of cities, while builders saw it as a chance to practise new techniques, and the government actively promoted it. In 1956, the Minister of Housing was concerned that local councils were not building blocks of flats high enough, despite the subsidies which were offered to encourage them, so a subsidy was introduced which increased with the number of storeys per block. The Minister explained to the House of Commons that the previous subsidies had 'unintentionally influenced local authorities to concentrate on building blocks of three, four or five storeys, which I believe many Honourable Members will agree are most monotonous'. We have since learnt that what Members of Parliament like the look of is not necessarily what suits the people who have to live there.

But height is only one aspect of housing, and there are many post-war council estates that have no high-rise houses but which nevertheless are generally agreed to have gone badly wrong. Typical of the worst of these is an estate built in the 1960s as part of Manchester's slum clearance programme: the Hulme Crescents. These long concrete blocks of maisonettes are badly designed, and do not provide what their tenants need. The open spaces between them are bleak and windswept. Most of the flats are now damp, cold and in bad repair; the tenants have called for them to be demolished and for traditional brick houses to be built in their place. The contrast with the council's dream of what the estate was meant to be is extreme. The architectural and planning partnership of Hugh Wilson and Lewis Womersley had been specially brought in to design the estate; Womersley wrote that the aim was 'to create an urban environment on a city scale. The solution to this problem . . . is to build continuous blocks of maisonettes at six-storeys high in a few bold and simple forms so as to develop large open spaces'. In designing crescents, he was recalling the beauty of architecture and housing layout of Georgian times.

'We feel that the analogy we have made with Georgian London and Bath is entirely valid. By the use of similar shapes and proportions, large-scale building groups and open spaces and, above all, by skilful landscaping and extensive tree planting, it is our endeavour to achieve, at Hulme, a solution to the problems of twentieth century living which would be the equivalent in quality of that reached for the requirements of the eighteenth century in Bloomsbury and Bath.'

Perhaps that is where the planners of Hulme went wrong. In trying to provide 'a solution to the problems of twentieth century living' which was not within their powers, they failed to achieve a more simple aim that was. Not that building satisfactory houses on a large scale is as simple as all that; it sometimes only seems that way because, with so many mistakes having been made in the past, we assume that we must have learnt from them. Perhaps the biggest mistake of all was to suppose that living communities could be built by standard methods and applied generally. There are no easy answers in making places for people to live in, but finding out what the people themselves want is a good way to start.

The disappointing results with many large-scale housing redevelopment schemes contributed to a move in the 1970s towards improving old houses rather than demolishing them. There was also a feeling that council officials were being over-enthusiastic in condemning whole streets of houses, and that the breaking up of communities in this way might be avoided. The government made grants available for installing the facilities that many old houses lack and for improving their immediate surroundings. In some areas, house improvement is now combined with demolishing a few of the worst houses, and perhaps replacing them with new ones. Large-scale redevelopment has become less fashionable now that it is accepted that an area can be improved or rebuilt gradually. Places are changing and growing older all the time, so there is no reason why their renewal should not be a continuous process. That is not a new idea, though it has sometimes been forgotten by planners. Perhaps something has been learnt from the recent history of urban renewal, but the dramatic swing in fashion from wholesale redevelopment to house improvement may not be permanent. Did the planners see the light, or did they merely lose their nerve and fall on financially hard times? If the latter is true then a return of confidence and spending power could some day bring the pendulum swinging back.

Fashions in town planning change, but their influence is small compared to the effects of changes in economic conditions. Changes in the economy have a direct influence on the physical form of towns and cities. In recent decades, for example, the industries on which the urban growth in the Industrial Revolution was based have declined. The docks, shipbuilding yards, engineering works and textile mills are being abandoned, while other activities – particularly service industries – have expanded, leading to offices being built in city centres on a large scale. But an unemployed docker is unlikely to retrain as a secretary in an insurance broker's office, so where can he fit in? Some people argue that he should move to wherever he can find a job, and that if a particular part of a town or city has ceased to fulfil the function for which it was originally created, we should not be afraid to accept that as an inevitable consequence of the constant process of urban change. This leads to local councils and their planners some-times accepting new development which does not provide the services or the type of employment that the area needs, but which seems to the council to be the only sort of development that is possible. Some argue that there is no point in trying to encourage new development to go to locations determined by an urban structure that was a response to the needs of a bygone age, and that a new structure suiting modern economic needs should be allowed to develop. If this means grassing over parts of the inner areas of our declining industrial cities, so be it.

Unfortunately, it is not as simple as that. When the economy of the inner area of a city declines, many young people and their families will move to a place that can provide a job and more pleasant surround-ings. The people who remain are those who are less likely to find a job somewhere else and will include the old, the disabled and the un-skilled. An inner city area cannot be abandoned overnight, and, if it is allowed to decline, living conditions will become increasingly unpleasant. As the population falls, it will no longer be able to support the facilities – shops, schools, and so on – that the remaining inhabitants need; and with a bleak economic future, the area's physical fabric will decay.

In recent years this process had led to some criticism of the new towns programme. Part of the original aim of the new towns was to relieve the overcrowding in large cities, and many people and some firms moved to new towns as a result. By the 1970s, in the light of increasing concern about the rapid decline of cities, fears were being expressed – particularly by politicians representing inner city areas – that the process had gone too far. Inner city populations have fallen to a level at which the survival of some communities is now threatened, and firms are closing at an alarming rate. This, some say, is partly the fault of the new towns: supported by public money, they attract people and businesses away from the inner cities, sucking out their life-blood.

If that analysis were correct, it would point to a simple solution to part of the inner city problem. But people do not need to be seduced from the inner cities by new towns – they leave willingly in search of work, housing and a better environment. Of those who do leave, only a small proportion go to the new towns. The majority add to the pressure for new development in the suburbs and on the outskirts of smaller towns and villages. As for the inner city firms which close, few of them move to new towns. Most cease to exist because changing economic conditions make them no longer profitable enough to survive. Supporters of new towns point out that the old inner cities cannot provide the conditions that many modern industries want, and they argue that if new economic activities are to flourish, and if industrial investment is to be attracted from multinational companies which can choose not only the location, but even the country which suits a particular new development, we must go out of our way to provide what they want: and the well-planned new towns, they say, are in a better position to do that.

Urban areas have a remarkable capacity for renewing themselves when the circumstances are right. Areas of old houses in bad condition are sometimes transformed in only a few years when they become fashionable and have a secure future. Wealthier owners move in and spend money improving their property, and house prices rise. Under these circumstances the life of a house can be prolonged almost indefinitely: there is no part that cannot be repaired or replaced. It is difficult to identify all the factors that lead to a particular area being upgraded in this way. Some may be in the control of the planners – by designating an area as one in which special house improvement grants are available, for example. But the effects of area improvement are mixed. The condition of the houses improve, but the housing conditions of the people who lived there originally may not. As prices rise, the people who were able to live in the area when it was run down – and therefore cheap – may find themselves having to look for less expensive accommodation elsewhere. It is not surprising that planners and councillors sometimes feel that urban renewal would be easy if it were not for the people.

The secret – which a lot of planners have still to learn – is that people are not the problem, but the solution. When Glasgow council first tried to improve tenement houses, it used to buy up an entire tenement block (by compulsory purchase if necessary), move the residents out, and then rehabilitate the whole block and let it to council tenants. In this way the houses were improved; but it often meant that they were left empty for a long time while the last few owner-occupiers in the block were forced out (much of the worst tenement housing in Glasgow is owner-occupied). Meanwhile the community was dispersed and destroyed. That was unfortunate, said the council, but there was no alternative. Or was there? A few people with imagination experimented with a new approach and eventually persuaded the authorities to apply it to thousands of Glasgow's old houses. Under this scheme, the agent of improvement is not the district council, but a specially created local housing association which is controlled and run – with the help of paid staff – by the people who live in the area and is supported by the Housing Corporation. Twenty of these community-based housing associations are now operating in Glasgow. They have shown that the city's tenements can be rehabilitated for the benefit of the community. What has been achieved by constructive community action has far exceeded the expectations of what community organisations can do. The Glasgow experience is strong evidence that giving communities a leading role is a key to successful urban renewal.

In the same way that momentum for renewal can build up, so can a spiral of decay. 'Planning blight' is the process in which public knowledge of plans for an area can lead to that area's decline, even before the plan is put into effect. For example, if the authorities decide that they will build a road through a particular area of houses at some future date, that area is likely to deteriorate: owners will see little point in paying to keep in good repair a house that is soon to be demolished. But planning is an uncertain business, and it is not uncommon for development proposals to be abandoned – sometimes after causing blight for years. Sensitive councils can minimise this by careful planning, but some councils have used blight as a tactic to clear the way for certain planning proposals of their own – which they might

Figure 7　Houses and shops boarded up may be the first sign that a neighbourhood is doomed (Rita van Capperen)

otherwise have had to scrap in the face of public opposition and the lack of any technical justification. Such cases usually concern an area of housing which stands in the way of the council's proposals for a road or a town centre development, for example. The trick is simple: the council first buys a few houses in the area and boards up or demolishes them. The streets soon begin to look as if they have no future, and the area starts to deteriorate. Residents who want to leave the dying community sell their homes to the council – no one else will buy them – and these are boarded up as well. Eventually the council is able to demolish the whole area on the grounds that the housing is of too poor quality to save, and there is then no obstacle to its own plans for the site. The planning system does have safeguards, but an unscrupulous council – or an unscrupulous commercial developer – can get away with a lot. There is no substitute for people keeping a close eye on what is happening in their area: a single boarded house could be the beginning of the end.

Sometimes the reasons for the downward spiral of decay are less easy to understand. Experts disagree about why one particular housing estate is unpopular and vandalised, while another built at the same time and to the same design is popular and in better condition. Much is written about the effects on people of the design of their houses, but more important influences on a housing estate are sometimes less obvious factors. The number of resident caretakers on an estate may be crucial, and the council's allocation policies – which decide who qualifies for a house on a particular part of an estate, and whether a particular part of an estate is earmarked as a place to dump families that the council considers to be trouble-makers – are often a key to the community's future.

Whatever the true reasons for the problems of urban areas, much is blamed on the planners. The term 'the planners' is often applied to anyone in a public position who makes decisions about the environment – including councillors, architects and road engineers, as well as professional town planners. Professional planners get more blame than they deserve, being held responsible for matters over which they have no control. To some extent they bring that on themselves. All professions try continuously to carve a bigger role for their members, and town planning – which does not look much like a profession even at the best of times – does so by claiming responsibility for more than it ought. The effect of this is to make it difficult for the public to see which matters are technical – and can therefore be left to the professionals – and which are questions of policy and opinion, which should be open to public debate. In obscuring the distinction, planners make it less likely that such decisions will be taken democratically.

But the overriding reason why major decisions affecting the environment are not taken democratically has nothing to do with planners. The outcome of battles over the environment depends largely on who has the economic muscle. It would take more than the planning system to change the direction in which Britain's economy is restructuring itself, and it is that restructuring process which is the main influence behind the changing face of Britain's towns and cities. Planning affects many important details, but it is a mistake to suppose that anyone is in a position to control the overall direction of urban development. Almost any piece of land over whose future use different interests are competing will provide a setting in which powerful economic interests can be seen using their weight to ensure that – whatever the planners may want – their own interests prevail.

That does not sound encouraging for people who want to have a say in their environment, but the warning should persuade them to get involved only on their own terms. From the orthodox perspective, the prospects for Britain's declining cities look bleak. The way that land is valued in the interests of the large financial institutions can mean that even when there is little competition for the use of a particular derelict inner city site, the price can remain high, so potential users of the land will be unable to save it from remaining waste. The big bureaucracies apply big bureaucratic solutions to urban problems, and they fail partly because they are inflexible. But when people who live in inner city areas have tackled the same problems in their own way, they have produced some impressive results. Community groups have drawn up plans that are realistic, technically competent, and have public support. They have improved houses, built workshops, run play schemes, and converted waste land into allotments and city farms. New life has been breathed into local branches of political parties, making councils more responsive to local needs. There have been determined challenges to the forces which transform urban areas without considering the people who live there.

The rate of success is often low, but the effort is essential. At stake is the extent to which changes to the environment will be democratically controlled – in so far as that is possible within the limits imposed by the present lack of democratic control over the economy. Unless democracy is constantly renewed from the bottom – by the active involvement of ordinary people – it will decay from the top through the abuse of political power. People are not the problem, but the solution.

Further reading

J B Cullingworth, *Town and Country Planning in Britain*, Allen & Unwin, 1979. A standard textbook on the planning system.

P Hall, *Urban and Regional Planning*, Penguin, 1975. The story of the development of planning in Britain and abroad.

A Ravetz, *Remaking Cities*, Croom Helm, 1980. The story of the development of town planning, its successes and failures, and an analysis of necessary changes in direction.

J M Simmie, *Citizens in Conflict: the Sociology of Town Planning*, Hutchinson, 1974. A description of town planning's social and political context.

4 Agriculture and Food Production

Jim Hall

As man evolved, so he ceased to be nomadic, and to forage for his food. Settled communities developed, which in turn necessitated the introduction of agriculture, that is farming or the art and practice of growing food, to supply his needs. Agriculture involves mechanical processes, such as the preparation of good soil conditions in which a planted seed may grow, the care of that plant as it grows, its proper feeding, weeding, protection from pests and diseases, and, when it reaches maturity, its harvesting, safe storage and marketing. It is a profession of great complexity, and in one chapter one should aim to do no more than whet the reader's appetite to search for more information on the subject.

In producing food the farmer is harnessing growth. This biological process has been manipulated by careful selection and cross-breeding of crops and animals so that now not only are, for example, quantities of wheat, barley, oats and many other grains, pulses, oilseeds and fibre crops grown that were undreamed of thirty years ago, but the farmer grows them for more precise uses. He can grow one wheat, with a highly complex chemical structure, that is suitable for bread making, another variety more suitable for biscuit making, and yet another one is used as a component of animal feeds. These animals process primary products – grains, pulses and grasses – and so provide us with a varied diet of milk, butter, cheeses, meat, bacon, eggs, and all the different foods which are found on the supermarket shelves. Agriculture is therefore an essential industry vital to our future since we must all eat to live.

It is not always realised that farming accounts for the main use of the countryside, controlling 83 per cent of this country's land, and using it as the 'factory floor' of a highly complex business requiring considerable skills. We shall see how farming has influenced the appearance of the countryside in the past and continues to do so today. (By contrast, less than 1 per cent of the countryside is influenced by considerations of nature conservation alone.)

Historical background

Let us look at the past so as to be better informed about the present.

The mystery of the missing link remains unsolved. If our ancestors were the primates (the ape families), then they were part of the wildlife around them. Our recognisable ancestor, *homo sapiens* (the thinking man), evolved gradually from the hunter searching for his food supplies, to the herdsmen domesticating wild animals and pasturing them where he knew they could be found when wanted; and from a random searcher for berries and roots, to the primitive farmer of clearings in the forest. The selection and breeding of crops and animals had begun: a simple process of adapting wildlife to man's needs.

Lightning, and the fire which might follow, must have provided the first dramatic opportunity for man and beast alike. It let light into the dark forests which originally covered this country. With light came fresh growth, where animals could find fresh food, and the apeman hunters, the animals. Perhaps one of our ancestors, brighter than average, saw the possibilities for further improvement. The rise of naturally occurring tools, such as pointed sticks, deer antlers for pick axes, flint arrowheads for spears, axes for knives, was followed, in turn, by the discovery and use of bronze and then iron, so man gradually evolved further and further from his primitive beginnings. It meant an improvement in his standard of living, an increase in his life expectancy and started the slow rise in population which in turn led to a greater need for food and so a need to convert more and more of the natural countryside to his specific needs. Food was the first priority – which meant clearing land on which to grow it; warmth and shelter came next, using the fuel and building material naturally to hand – trees from the forest for both fires and dwellings, then later for wooden ships. Much later still the beginning of the Industrial Revolution, built on iron and charcoal, demanded yet more timber from the forest. Thus the countryside was rapidly changed – the increase in the population may have been the single largest cause of change, the need for food the prime motivation, but people also needed housing and protection. Solitary huts grew into settlements, some settlements into towns. Rutted farm tracks have now become motorways, pastures have become airports. Leisure and ease of travel have brought the countryside within reach of the townsman, all bringing additional pressure on a diminishing asset, and acting as additional agents of change.

Now let us put some figures to population changes.

When the Domesday survey was made in 1080 the population of this country was estimated at 1½ million people. By 1349 it exceeded 3½ million, only to be halved in that year by the Black Death. By 1700 it had climbed to 7 million and one hundred years later it had shot up to 42 million. Today we are more concerned with population growth on a world-wide basis than with just our own 54 million. Add to sheer numbers the increased expectancy of life in the UK, from forty-four years in the nineteenth century to today's seventy-five years, and we see how population pressures have grown.

Farming populations by contrast have declined. Like all industries farming has become capital – rather than labour-intensive, machines taking over a lot of manual work, and chemicals replacing the countless labourers hoeing and pulling weeds. In 1963 there were 227,000 farmers employing 976,000 farmhands; in 1980 these are down to 190,000 and 510,000 respectively, and their numbers are still falling. Every five years farming is being lost to urban development at a rate equivalent to one-third of the area of the county of Gloucestershire; the remaining farming land is now owned by fewer farmers, again following the modern trend for larger and (questionable though it may be) more efficient units.

Changes in tenure are also worth studying. Primitive man defended his territory. The eleventh-century Norman lords were given huge estates and rights which they imposed and maintained by might, over the land and the men who lived on it. Since the introduction of death duties in the nineteenth century the large estates have been broken up and many tenant farmers were, and still are, able to buy and become owner-occupiers and managers of land. And more recently yet another new owner is emerging – the insurance company, or pension fund, using their capital resources to buy a stake in the land and planning for a good return on their investment.

Pressure has also arisen within farming itself. When the village was supplied exclusively by surrounding farms they needed to provide bread and meat, apples and milk, beer and cider, grown on the spot. The resulting mixed-farming system and crop rotation used the ample labour available, and maintained a certain level of crop fertility and animal health. Now the tendency is for simpler systems – corn in the east where the terrain and climate is more favourable; sheep, beef and dairying in the west where the higher rainfall gives rise to good conditions for grass growth, and upland areas are utilised to best advantage.

Nor should we forget the changes which the building of roads, industrial sites and airports have made to the countryside. Today's farmer produces over 50 per cent of our total food requirements and in some products, such as liquid milk, all our needs, thanks to more productive strains of crops, improved drainage systems and enhanced pest and disease control.

Agriculture and countryside change

But what changes has farming made to the countryside? Again we should not forget what has happened physically and historically, nor man's attitude to nature and to wilderness. To biblical man Paradise was a benevolent land flowing with milk and honey, not a wilderness: it is reported that the Pilgrim Fathers, setting foot on America from *The Mayflower* were appalled at what they found. They feared their new environment and had reason to: it was a hostile place in which man had to protect himself from wildlife. Yet over a comparatively few generations their successors have tamed that wilderness from the Atlantic across three thousand miles to the Pacific.

In this country the time scale for change was much longer. In the south-west, where the Celts settled, land around the family homesteads tended to be enclosed by walls or hedges; while in the Midlands and the east, which are more climatically suited to cereals, the tendency was towards the open field system, where the lord of the manor controlled communal ownership which tilled, fallowed and grazed in rotation. Between the villages were the 'wastes', which were used for grazing, but which also harboured outlaws.

Social historians disagree about what happened from then on and in this chapter it is only possible to convey a general sense of the changes that took place. Enclosure of both 'field' and 'waste' started under the Tudors, enforced by legislation and generally favouring existing and newly-emerged power groups. Many poor people were displaced from land which once supported them; but it was not all bad. It marked the end of the feudal system, which held many to one village and one occupation for life, and so provided an opportunity for the industrious and enterprising yeoman farmers to compete with the rich and established landowners, and resulted in improved production and an increase in the overall standard of living.

The enclosure movement reached its peak during the eighteenth century so that by 1820 the 'agricultural revolution' was fully evident in the chequerboard of small hedged fields which today we think of as the 'natural' countryside. Comparatively little pre-historic country-side remained and this only because it was too difficult or too unproductive to reclaim for agricultural use or was necessary for timber production or to provide cover for game.

A study of the Amberden parish maps (pp. 46 and 47) illustrates this change and also the next phase of change, the removal of the hedges. Hedges became redundant in some areas with the change from mixed farming to more simple arable systems. The great forests had gone long ago, and concern is now expressed for the disappearing hedgerow. The woodland relics of the old forests are also threatened. Since they no longer produce timber and have no great lord protecting them for hunting, many have been cleared to grow crops. Piped water, much less of a disease risk for cattle, has replaced the ponds, which, passing out of use, are now also targets for reclamation. At one stage it began to look as though progress would mean the gradual disappearance of all natural areas (or habitats so called), until science combined with a nostalgia for the passing of an era (largely seen, but very loosely defined, as the height of the enclosure movement in the eighteenth century), began to ask whether a line should not be drawn at which progress must be halted. The more emotive of those people voicing alarm, the conservationists, went further, and demanded not only that such a line be drawn, but that legislation be passed to enforce their views, and they continue to do so. Such legislation forms a subject of its own.

It became more and more evident that a wide range of interests had to be taken into account before our various needs could be reconciled. It must be repeated that we all need food, farmers' livelihoods are involved, progress continues with scientific research and develop-ment into crop and stock production and even if the importance of conserving the countryside and all that that signifies becomes in-

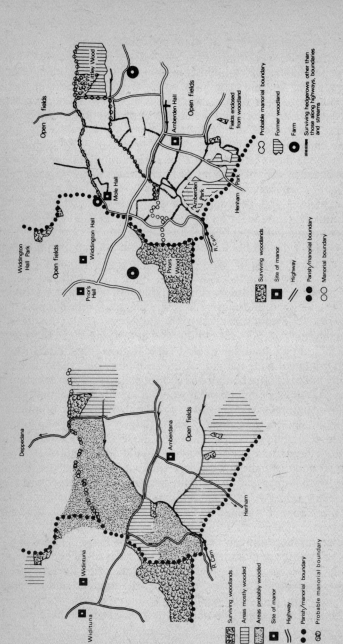

Figure 8   Domesday Amberden, Essex

Figure 9   Medieval Amberden and Mole Hall

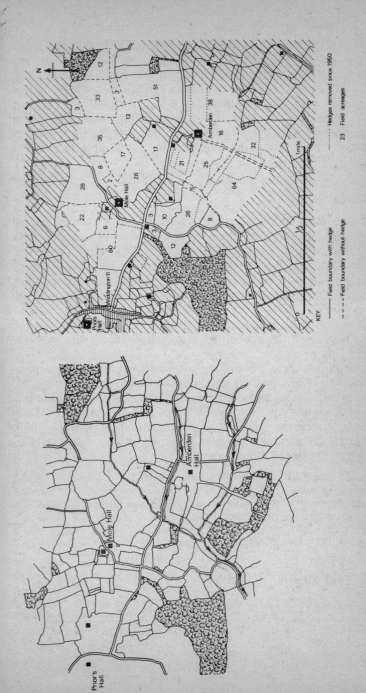

Figure 10 Amberden in 1839

Figure 11 Amberden Farm in 1976

KEY

—— Field boundary with hedge ········ Hedges removed since 1950

– – – Field boundary without hedge 23 Field acreages

creasingly apparent, it is still a confused issue. What can be said is that we are now moving towards a consensus of opinion within farming circles, as well as without, that whilst we can never halt progress, it must be pursued with due regard to the safeguarding of natural resources (wildlife and landscape to some, biological safety for the future to others). This need is accepted. Deciding the measure of how much, where and how is going to exercise the minds of farmer, scientist, the general public and politicians alike for a long time to come.

Conservation

It is time to consider what is meant by the term conservation. For too long, and assisted by the media, we have equated conservation with rare and exotic species, with nature reserves and sites of special scientific interest. Now it has become apparent that we have a more serious problem on our hands than the extinction of just a few species. It may be no exaggeration to say that amongst today's many perils to human survival may be the gradual and insidious disappearance of our natural resources. The gospel for survival may now have to be the security of plenitude, not only the last ditch stand for rarity preservation.

This is inextricably bound up with the need for food at a price people can afford; with progress, which means the technology of systems, machines, and chemicals; with the fact that farming is a business and has to pay its way. Thus, any definition of 'conservation' must have meaning to farmer, scientist, society and politician alike. Credit for the definition of conservation which does this goes to an ecologist, Charles Elton, who said:

> Unless one thinks that man was intended to be an all-conquering and sterilising power in the world there must be some general basis for understanding what it is best to do. This means looking for some wise principle of co-existence between man and nature, even if it has to be a modified kind of man and a modified kind of nature. That is what I understand by CONSERVATION.

The task ahead

If, following Elton, we look at the conservationist's point of view we find a near desperate case made for the complete preservation of the special sites, nature reserves and areas of high scientific interest, with comparatively few resources diverted to looking after general conservation – the safeguarding of plenitude, as I described it earlier.

If, on the other hand, we consider the question from the farmer's viewpoint and under the pressures in which he operates, we find a curious dichotomy. There is a wide appreciation that a proportion of natural species, and an element of beauty, should be left, but some farmers may still believe that there is still too much land being 'wasted' and that the right action is to turn it to agricultural use, by draining and ploughing, or felling and clearing according to whether it is wetland, moor or woodland. The farmer's customer, the general public (or the way government acts on its behalf) seems to endorse that view. Grants are paid to encourage reclamation of the very areas which the statutory conservation organisations have advised the same politicians are becoming rare and therefore need protection. A number of steps are now urgently needed. They have been obvious for so long that some feel that they should be indelibly stamped on every heart.

Instead of the coldly 'of scientific interest', or 'because we have a statutory duty to do so' on the one hand, and the emotional appeal of furry little animals or colourful birds on the other (some of which will be busy eating farmers' crops), we need a calm statement on the fundamental need to safeguard natural resources. Recognising that natural resources, plants, animals, sound and colour, all help to form an attractive landscape, we need to help the visiting townsman to appreciate and treasure all that he sees on his visits to the countryside, *including* the farming which goes on and which gives it life and purpose.

One great impediment to linking progress and conservation is successive governments' five-year terms of office for thought and action, for most decisions are political. We need to replace the idea of 'the next five years' with 'in perpetuity', for that is how long we must look for life to go on. Unless we do so, we wittingly or unwittingly rob our successors of the resources which we should have held in trust for them. It may appear as a moral issue, and so it should, but it is an intensely practical one at the same time. Farmers, and the scientists who serve them, whether as advisers or in research, have to learn to take a broader view, and to take it longer term as well. Would it not be wise for them to ponder the future? We have increased yields immensely but it has been on the basis of 'have identified enemy, will proceed to kill'. Pests and controlling predators alike have been reduced, but whereas pests abound and proliferate, their predators are steadily being eradicated. There are signs of an awareness of the dangers attached to this simplistic approach, both to agriculture and to the natural environment, but no general acceptance as yet.

Where, how and why?

Suppose, then, that the calm statement which I called for earlier has been made and generally accepted. There will still be the problem of how, when and where even if the why is generally accepted. For a start there will be special areas whose protection must have high priority; some are already owned and managed by various conservation bodies, both statutory and voluntary, but many are still owned and managed by farmers and landowners.

Must they all be run for ever as they are now? The conservation bodies find their management of reserves costly. What should the farmer do if his general economic state prevents him from continuing the low intensity of production, as with grazing flower-rich, old meadows for example, or his very survival depends on increasing production? In very few instances, under today's public approach to conservation, is goodwill supported by practical and financial aid. Nevertheless, while there may be a shortage of practical aid this is the popular idea of conservation, involving as it does the emotion and excitement of rallying to the protection of wildlife and landscape threatened, so popular jargon has it, by 'greedy and unthinking farmers'.

A lack of practical and financial aid and an emotive approach, containing within it seeds of destruction, must not blind us to the scientific reasons for protection for these high priority areas. They are special areas which have been created by past generations, mostly of farmers who were not thinking of conservation, who saw no other way of managing their land, and no other reason for acting in any other way. They fall into the very category which once lost are gone for good; they cannot be recreated. They are often relict areas left because in pre-conservation days they were areas that were too difficult to drain; heathlands that without today's fertilisers were not rewarding enough to farm; woodlands that were once preserved for timber and sporting interests by the old estates, now seen as useless by new owners; upland moors of special value to both plant and bird life, but viewed by foresters as ripe for afforestation with conifers. The case for preserving a selection of such sites (possibly all of them – who knows?)

is self-evident to some but not by any means to all those who own them and see in them an unwarranted curb on their freedom of action – a freedom which they sometimes see as needed for their own personal survival. This approach does not make the owners any greedier than men in other walks of life, and if they are somewhat reluctant then it is because farming priorities are difficult to displace by conservation priorities, especially when faced with that psychological barrier of believing that the conservationist, rather than conservation, is gaining at the farmers' expense.

So much for the priority view of countryside conservation. The second way of looking at the countryside concerns the 99 per cent of the countryside where food production has to have priority. Nevertheless there are great possibilities for saving the best of the old landscape and wildlife features, even if not all of them.

Every farm has areas of landscape and wildlife. There will be special pockets of interest – rarities to protect, and other degrees of importance all the way down to the common and plentiful. There will also be wildlife, for which cropping has provided a special niche, which, when it reaches pest status, has to be managed (the rabbit for instance). Care for the countryside will be concerned with viability, with managing pests, but without causing unnecessary change or destruction. The areas on farms which concern us are worth listing:

— field boundaries, hedges, banks, walls and fences;
— shelter-belts, windbreaks, copses and woodland;
— scrub, heaths and moorland;
— access areas, roads, tracks, bridleways, footpaths and their verges;
— areas around farm buildings, stockyards, machinery storage grounds;
— odd rough grassy areas, embankments and steep slopes, small paddocks;
— wet areas, bogs, marshes, ponds, lakes, reservoirs, slurry pits;
— running water, streams, brooks, ditches;
— marl pits, old chalk pits, quarries, disused railway lines.

Without knowing exactly what plant, bird, insect or mammal will be found there you can safely assume that all these areas will have some form of wildlife. This is easier to understand if you remember that the term wildlife covers *all* living things that are not cultivated or domesticated, so the plants in the hedgerow and the trees in the wood are a form of wildlife as well as the yellowhammers, partridges, or red admiral butterflies that live in them. It also includes soil microorganisms, many of which play a part in crop production. In most cases these areas will either form part of the farm's necessary functions, such as the roadway verge, the ditches and the streams, or they will be of marginal value, such as wet hollows difficult to drain, steep banks and ponds. Whatever category they fall into, management now means a plan. For a start there has to be a balance between productive and unproductive areas: the farm or estate must pay, that is common sense. Having put first things first, it should still be possible to leave enough wildlife and landscape features to form an acceptable countryside. It will be different from the landscape of even thirty years ago, and dependent on a general public/farmer understanding of viability linked to countryside care.

Some would see this approach as paring the countryside to the very bone, whereas we know there is a large element of choice. A reasonable maximum field size may well be twenty hectares. Some such decision should be made and adhered to, otherwise hedges will ultimately disappear, but there are still 8- or 12-hectare fields aplenty. There are farmers who pursue maximum profitability as though driven by some irresistible force, even though they may have to pay the Inland Revenue a good percentage of it. Others will farm just as well but enjoy their woods and their sport, their primroses, owls or sparrow-hawks. Others again will have so little vision as to dump tins and tyres in their ponds, yet others will keep them clean and take pride in every thing that grows and moves there.

Such countryside planning and management now involves the day-to-day operations on the farm. It will even – and this may be news to some – involve the choice of chemicals to use, and certainly indicate a very careful assessment of when to spray and not to spray. Apart from spending money unnecessarily, pests become resistant to the chemicals, while their predators are reduced, and then the pests can proliferate. Nor should it ever be forgotten that we are now using some highly poisonous chemicals which are equally dangerous to man.

Rehabilitation

The third way of caring for the countryside comes under the heading of 'rehabilitation'. Sometimes it may be motivated by a twinge of conscience for past actions, sometimes to improve working surroundings, at other times to improve sporting prospects. It may be linked to new works, such as making the irrigation reservoir into an attractive and interesting area through properly profiling the bottom and introducing water vegetation. It may be planting trees, or even the planting of hedges. Ponds have been created for their own sake – though they have an ancillary use as a fire-fighting reserve of water. Nesting boxes have been fixed to trees. My beliefs have recently been supported by a joint statement issued by the National Farmers' Union and Country Landowners' Association in which they declare that their members should accept a responsibility for caring for the countryside. I believe too that society must accept that it has its part to play and that priorities must be established.

Confusions

In this chapter I have argued that the primary use of land must be for food production, but not everyone agrees. At present there are surpluses of food within the EEC and there is a body of opinion which says that we no longer need to devote as much land to food production as hitherto.

Another opinion states that we should use our land to its full potential and export food to those parts of the world which are hungry. Yet another expert tells us that if we ceased the wasteful process of feeding cereals and pulses to animals we could use the products saved to feed humans; we would be able to feed ourselves on less land and so would not need to drain our marshes, plough up our moorland, or use chemicals to increase production. There may be some merit in all these suggestions, but the economic difficulties of such radical changes to our farming systems, the difficulties of world-wide distribution and of changing dietary tastes and prejudices, lead to such confusion that it is suggested that they are for the future, not the present.

The Farming Wildlife Advisory Service

Is anything being done about these conflicting views? In 1967 a small group of farmers and conservationists got together to consider why such animosity was being expressed against farming change and why there was such a reaction by farmers against what they regarded as unfair and unwarranted criticism. No one body, they discovered, was charged with evaluating agricultural change. No one to consider whether anything needed to be done, or, if something had to be done, to carry out the necessary work. Their first step was to test the effects of change in a practical farm study. For the first time, the wildlife – trees, shrubs, plants, birds, insects etc. – was surveyed beforehand. This information was included in planning the future of a farm. Now known as the 'Silsoe exercise', it showed that whilst changes had to be made to make a farm viable, these could be carried out without the 'devastation' that was taking place in farm 'improvements' generally. A mixed company of 100 farmers, landowners, agricultural advisers, members of both the statutory and voluntary conservation bodies, people of status – joined in the planning. They also joined in discussion and in an exchange of points of view. It was an historic occasion which marked a change in thinking in both agriculture and conservation circles.

It lead to the formation of the Farming and Wildlife Advisory Group (FWAG) which has since grown until it now has groups in forty-one counties. FWAG, formed as an independent body covering farming, landowning and conservation interests, then stated its objectives. These were to identify the problems of reconciling the needs of modern farming with the conservation of nature and the landscape which supports it; to explore areas of compromise, and to make the results of this work as widely known as possible. They came to the conclusion that, since in the British Isles land use planning of over 80 per cent of the country's surface is in the hands of farmers and landowners, whereas less than 1 per cent is planned with conservation specifically in mind, farmers' attitudes and their belief or not in the value of conservation were all important, in fact crucial. They expressed the opinion that unless we can arrive at an accepted consensus of 'what it is best to do' on this land, the special areas, such as nature reserves and sites of special scientific interest, will become museum islands in a sea of indifference, and our countryside deteriorate into a monotony of crops, and the pests and diseases which prey on them. What was once described as a 'disequilibrium in nature' will prevail.

FWAG realises that an accepted consensus will not happen spontaneously. Dialogue, discovery and discussion must lead to decisions which may not always achieve the maximum desirable effect but should strive for the best possible. And these decisions must then be put into practice.

Further reading

Caring for the Countryside, National Farmers' Union, 1977. This four-page leaflet suggests Conservation Guidelines and Action Points for farmers, while also pointing out that the land is the backcloth to life and the most important resource in the business of agriculture.

E S Carter and R B Sayce, 'Conservation of Agricultural Land', in *Journal of the Royal Agricultural Society of England*, Volume 140, 1979. An objective view of the agricultural scene written by two prominent Government scientists.

Farming and Wildlife: A Study in Compromise, the report of the Silsoe Exercise, Royal Society for the Protection of Birds, 1969. The proceedings of a weekend conference when farmers and conservationists met to plan the future of a Hertfordshire farm, matching the needs of agriculture with those of wildlife.

Nature Conservation and Agriculture, Nature Conservancy Council, 1977. An appraisal of the effects of agricultural progress on nature conservation with some proposals for future action.

New Agricultural Landscapes, Countryside Commission, 1974. This report discusses the landscape changes brought about by agricultural developments, with reference to study areas in lowland Britain.

Sinews for Survival: A Report on the Management of Natural Resources, HMSO, 1972. This study was conducted in connection with the United Nations Conference on the Human Environment which took place in Stockholm in 1972; the subjects covered by eminent people in their field included agriculture, wildlife, transport and recreation.

Peter Wormell, *Anatomy of Agriculture*, Harrap, 1978. An informative study of present-day agriculture which deals with technology while emphasising that agriculture is a business which has to keep abreast of progress.

5 Woodlands and Forestry

George Peterken

Britain has about 2000 kha (thousands of hectares) of woodland, but in 1895 the Board of Agriculture recorded only 1104 kha. In the twentieth century, therefore, woodland in the UK has almost doubled from 5 to 9 per cent of the land surface. Even this rapid expansion still leaves us low in the European league, where most countries have more than 20 per cent woodland; and we have to import 92 per cent of the timber we consume (at a cost of £2750 million in 1979). Home timber production will increase as the massive new plantations come 'on stream'. Even so, if recent predictions are correct, Britain will still produce much less than half of the timber we are expected to consume in 2050. Meanwhile as much as 300 kha of woodland, now classified as unproductive by the Forestry Commission, are not directly influenced by the techniques and assumptions of modern forestry.

Behind these statistics lies a tale of profound and rapid change. Woodlands, which had remained largely unaltered since the twelfth century, have been destroyed or transformed. Huge tracts of moorland, which had been virtually treeless for centuries, have been covered by conifer plantations. Traditional practices evolved over centuries have been abandoned in a few decades, and replaced by modern, energy-intensive, mechanised methods which differ fundamentally in practical, social and economic characteristics. Just as 'agri-business' has displaced traditional farming, so modern forestry has supplanted traditional woodmanship and sheep husbandry, and thereby created environmental problems which we are still far from solving.

Existing woodland and recent changes

The latest Forestry Commission census in 1965 revealed that half Britain's 1743 kha of woodland consisted of conifer plantations (see Table 1, below). Most were stocked with introduced species, such as Sitka spruce, Norway spruce, larch and lodgepole pine; only 28 per cent of the total area was occupied by Scots pine, our main native timber-producing conifer, and most of this had been planted well beyond its native range in Britain. Almost all the conifer plantations dated from after 1920: before 1920 few had been established and most of those which had, would have been ready for felling by 1965. Broadleaf high forest, on the other hand, was mostly much older – 77 per cent dated from before 1920, and 28 per cent was over a century

Table 1 Area of major woodland types in Britain in 1965 and 1977 (thousands of hectares)*

	1965	1977
Coniferous high forest: mainly even-aged plantations.	918	1312
Broadland high forest: mainly plantations of broadleaves, and broadleaves mixed with conifers; also a small proportion of coppice promoted to high forest.	350	348
Coppice and coppice-with-standards: stands still cut in rotation or not long overdue for cutting.	30	47
Scrub and felled woodland: mainly long-neglected coppice.	445	290
Total	1743	1997

*Derived from Forestry Commission sources. (Note that changes in the exact definition of categories hampers direct comparison of results for the two dates.)

old – and mostly consisted of native species, principally oak and beech. However, most broadleaf woodland was classified as coppice and scrub, the residue of traditional woodland management.

Since 1965 the trends established earlier in the twentieth century have continued unabated. Conifers now dominate two-thirds of all British woodland. The increase has come mainly by planting on upland moors, but also by felling broadleaf coppice and high forest and planting conifers in their place. Between 1965–79 conifers never formed less than 98.5 per cent of *all* Forestry Commission plantings. In the lowlands, the trend to conifers was intensified by continued 'reclamation' of broadleaf woods to agriculture. By 1977, the 1707 kha of productive woodland were equally divided between the Forestry Commission and private growers (much of the private woodland was managed by companies such as the Economic Forestry Group and Fountain Forestry). The remaining 290 kha of unproductive (of timber) scrub and felled woodland were almost all in the hands of private individuals, local authorities, and organisations such as the National Trust.

Our task here is to consider the impact of forestry in conservation terms, and especially its impact on existing woodlands. Unfortunately, these considerations are notoriously complex: how, for example, should we regard an increase in the use of paper? Does it mean yet more destruction of scarce woodland, or possibly a better market for wood and thus a better chance that a wood will not be cleared for agriculture? We shall have to limit ourselves to selected issues.

Benefits from woodland

Woodlands yield a wide variety of benefits to society, and it is important to understand how they relate to each other in practice.

1 Timber

Wood is an important and renewable material resource. Timber is used in mines, in the paper-making industry, sawmills and factories manufacturing chipboard, fibreboard and wood wool. These products are used in construction, packaging, furniture and a wide range of minor products, such as tool handles. Wood is also a fuel and a source of distilled chemicals.

2 Pasturage and shelter for livestock

Small woods are important for sheep and deer in the uplands, but in the past deer and cattle were commonly depastured in woods in the lowlands.

3 Sport
Pheasants, foxes and woodcock are reared and sheltered especially in the small woods within farmland, and provide sport to the wealthy and possibly sporting rents to the landowner.

4 Landscape
Many of our most attractive landscapes owe much of their character to the presence of mature, broadleaf woodland, e.g. the Wye Valley on the Welsh borders and the fringes of the Lake District and Dartmoor National Parks. Even in the less spectacular countryside, woods and hedgerow trees are often the main bulwark against the spectre of arable prairies. The recent loss of millions of elms, formerly dominant features of the British countryside, due to the ravages of Dutch Elm disease, has illustrated graphically the importance of trees in the landscape, and the need for continual replanting.

5 Public access to the countryside
Woods provide a degree of seclusion for those who prefer more privacy than can be obtained on a popular beach. In the farmed countryside there may be few other places where one can walk without restriction.

6 History
Many woods have existed in the landscape for centuries in roughly their present form. They give almost as much character and identity to these places as the parish church, timber-framed cottages, and the village pond.

7 Nature conservation
Not only are woods generally rich in variety of habitat and wildlife species, but woodland is also the natural vegetation of much of Britain and therefore imbued with more ecological significance than, say, grasslands and heathlands, which have been derived from woodland.

It would be wonderful if all these benefits could be enjoyed in all woods all the time, but in practice there are limits to the compatibility of different activities. For example, gamekeepers prefer mature broadleaf woodland with open rides, glades, well-developed ground vegetation and some low shrubby cover – conditions which were admirably provided by the traditional coppice-with-standards system. The same system is valuable for nature conservation, which values the stability it provides as well as the variety of habitat, and the main difference of opinion concerns birds of prey. Public access is obviously not possible in a pheasant preserve, and decidedly risky in a wood where timber is being felled, but is completely compatible with landscape conservation.

The main problem lies in harmonising timber production with the maintenance of other benefits. Indeed, in its more intensive forms, involving mono-culture plantations of mainly alien, coniferous species, forestry is regarded by many as quite incompatible with other interests. The short rotations involve clear-felling woods just as they begin to mature in landscape terms, and the large patches of recently felled woods scar the view. The rigid organisation of plantation boundaries and planting lines inject an unwelcome artificiality into what might once have seemed a relatively natural scene. Conifer plantations provide poor cover for game during much of their growth cycle. Semi-natural communities are often destroyed in order to form plantations. The wildlife inside mono-culture plantations tends to be poor, which is hardly surprising since the target of the timber grower is to channel as much as possible of the energy and nutrient flows in the eco-system into timber production, not wildlife. Fortunately, the worst effects of this fundamental incompatibility between intensive timber growing and most other demands have been mitigated by two measures: 1) segregation of objectives, and 2) modification of forestry practice. These are discussed in the concluding sections, after we have considered four particular issues: forestry in the uplands, the choice of species, the treatment of semi-natural woods and the future of small woods.

Forestry in the uplands

The great expansion of British forestry this century has taken place largely in the uplands of north and west Britain, where previously almost treeless counties such as Nairn and Kirkcudbright have lately become more wooded than the traditionally well-wooded counties of south-east England. Huge expanses of montane grassland, heath and peatland, formerly used mainly as sheep pasture, have been fenced, ploughed and covered with conifers – mainly Sitka spruce, Scots pine, larch, Norway spruce, lodgepole pine and Douglas fir. If forestry continues to expand as planned, plantations will eventually cover some 30 per cent of the land surface of Scotland.

Change on this scale has inevitably generated hostility from several quarters. Forests intercept more rainfall than grassland so run-off from catchments is reduced by about 15 per cent and eventually more reservoirs are required. Forests tend to acidify stream water, and this is said to affect the quality of fishing. Plantations bring an obtrusive, organised element into scenery which was dominated by natural features; Highland scenery is unlike any other in Europe, but conifer plantations are reducing its distinctiveness. Ramblers object to both the landscape change and restrictions on access. Naturalists note how moorland waders, such as the golden plover, ravens and birds of prey depend on extensive *open* habitats, and do not regard the influx of small birds such as chaffinches and tits into plantations as adequate compensation. The loss of important semi-natural habitats, such as the raised mires of Lochar Moss in southern Scotland, is deplored. Conservationists are worried too at the possible long-term consequences of afforestation, which may be subject to increasing invertebrate pest outbreaks in mono-cultures, as well as accelerated soil erosion and loss of site fertility.

The biggest debate, however, concerns the general question of whether hill land is better grazing sheep or growing trees. Agricultural interests point out that Britain imports food as well as timber, and that expansion of forestry diminishes our capacity to feed ourselves. In practice, the relationship is not so straightforward, for land not appropriated by forestry may be capable of improvement as pasture, thus maintaining livestock yields. Indeed, there has long been talk of integrating farming and forestry in the uplands, i.e. each land-holding having a mixture of the two, with forestry on the poorer soil; roads, fences and other expensive items serving both interests; and improvement of yields from both activities with fertilisers. In practice, this has had only limited success because the Forestry Commission and the forestry management companies have tended to buy whole estates and convert them to forestry in their entirety. Economic comparisons are inconclusive and considerably affected by the levels of government aid, but there have been periods when hill farming has been rewarding enough to stem the flow of land into forestry.

Clearly, the various interests which criticise forestry in the uplands prefer the land to remain in hill farming. Foresters, not unnaturally, have responded by throwing doubt on criticisms which have not been carefully proved and then, when the proof has been forthcoming, they say that the disadvantages are the price one must pay for increased home timber production. Landscape objections have been partly met by planting to irregular boundaries and by shaping the areas of planting and felling to blend with the natural land form. Wildlife objections are sometimes met by not planting right up to stream sides and thus retaining some habitat diversity, and by pointing out that some wildlife species actually like plantations. Although many important semi-natural habitats have been damaged by forestry, the Forestry Commission has been prepared to sell land to conservation organisations when the objections to forestry have been strong. More subtly, promises of a better future are made: when the plantations mature we can expect a greater variety of species and structure.

Some indication of the complexity of the arguments can be gained from the various predictions about how the plantation will be treated in the future. Whilst some foresters look to mature spruce woods with a small-scale pattern of older and younger stands and an admixture of broadleaves, supporting a rich community of wildlife, accepted by the general public as stable and attractive features in the landscape, other foresters advocate quite the opposite, a kind of agri-silviculture in which dense, even, heavily fertilised, coniferous mono-cultures are grown for only 30–40 years, then harvested in great swathes like a field of barley. Conservationists instinctively react against the latter mechanised and energy-intensive prospect, but it is arguable that it will enable moorland wildlife to regain a temporary foothold in the forests, and that, in any case, short-lived conifer stands, periodically destroyed by gales or fire, would now be the natural state of the uplands.

Another issue concerns the distribution of future afforestation: Should it be in large blocks leaving large patches of upland untouched by forestry, or is it better to scatter forests around evenly in small patches? Here too the conservation arguments are uncertain. Small, scattered forests bring diversity of habitat locally, but all regions might come to look alike, and no area would be free of any damaging effects of forestry. 'Blanket afforestation' (large, dense forests) is often deplored by conservationists on the grounds that habitat variety is lost, but it does produce new landscape on a grand scale appropriate to the hill lands. As it happens, economic factors favour large-scale forestry and doubtless we shall see more forests develop like those at Kielder. The main problem lies in the unwillingness of forestry to accept planning restraints, which might enable new plantations to be sited with least damage to water resources, wildlife and famous landscapes which are admired in their present treeless condition.

Choice of species

When felled woodland is replanted (and indeed when open ground is afforested) the forester has a chance to determine which tree species will form the next stand or crop. If, as is usually the case, he is primarily interested in growing utilisable timber at a profit he will tend to select fast-growing species. In most instances this means conifers, which can usually produce 10–18 cubic metres of wood per hectare each year, far greater than broadleaves such as oak and beech, which achieve only 4–8m³ ha/yr. Oak timber is worth much more than conifer per unit volume, but this does not offset the benefits of rapid growth and consequent earlier harvesting of most conifers.

With commercial pressures like this it is hardly surprising that the rapid replacement of traditional coppicing by plantation forestry has been accompanied by a substantial amount of conifer planting where previously only broadleaves have grown. In Salcey Forest (Bucks and Northants), for example, only broadleaves were planted before 1943, but from 1943–60 conifers were commonly mixed with the broadleaves, and after 1960 large areas of pure conifers were planted. Even when broadleaves were planted there was a shift in the 1940s from the traditional oak and ash to beech, which is probably not a native tree in this site.

Unfortunately, the emphasis on conifers has its critics on broad conservation grounds. Conifers produce a heavy litter which, because it decomposes slowly, builds up on the forest floor and makes the soil more acid. On certain soil types, notably infertile acid sands and heavy wet clays, conifers may eventually produce irreversible soil changes and loss of fertility. The introduction of conifers into the landscape has had a mixed reception: on the whole they are welcomed in small clumps and as natural regeneration (e.g. pine on heathland) but deplored when, as is usually the case in woodland, they appear as blocks of uniform, even-aged, obviously artificial plantations in place of mature, apparently natural broadleaf stands. Conifers also have substantial effects on wildlife. Whilst a few species, such as goldcrests, are favoured, many others decline. Spring flowering herbs, such as the bluebell, anemone and primrose, cannot compete under the evergreen canopy. Numerous beetles, moths and other invertebrates use native broadleaf trees as homes and food plants, but far fewer use introduced conifers.

Not surprisingly, foresters have looked for alternative species which are more acceptable on environmental grounds, yet still grow reasonably fast. Larch has been favoured because it grows fairly fast like other conifers, yet has deciduous foliage which provides seasonal variety of colour in the landscape as well as spring light for bluebells, etc. Sycamore, a fairly productive deciduous broadleaf tree has been widely introduced, though it provides a poor habitat for wildlife. Recently, foresters have placed considerable hope in the so-called southern hemisphere beeches, *Nothofagus*, which have grown very fast in some parts of Britain yet still provide a good habitat for wildlife (both invertebrates and ground vegetation) and merge well with native broadleaves in the landscape.

When arguments arise over choice of species, the difficulties are sometimes not so much about the species themselves but more about the silvicultural treatment with which they are associated. For example, when a mature oakwood is felled and replaced with a Douglas fir plantation, do we object to the introduction of conifers, the substitution of old woodland by young woodland, the loss of apparently natural woodland to obviously artificial plantations, or simply to change itself? When, as sometimes happens, the public objects to the felling and replacement with oak of a mature oak plantation, the problems are clearly not associated with the species at all.

Treatment of semi-natural woodlands

Although 'semi-natural' cannot be defined precisely, the term embraces those woods which originated by natural regeneration or whose composition is broadly natural. In practice the term is limited to those woods which have not been planted, although borderline cases, such as a mature oak plantation on a site which would naturally support oak, are often accepted as semi-natural. No woods in Britain are completely natural, though there are still some virgin forests in central Europe where man has had only negligible influence.

Many woods are described as 'ancient'. Understandably this conjures up visions of aged, gnarled oaks and the like, though in fact age of trees is not directly involved. Ancient woods are simply those which existed in the Middle Ages and perhaps earlier. Surviving examples have therefore existed continuously for 400 years or more. Some do contain very old trees, but most have been felled and regenerated many times in their long history.

Six types of semi-natural woodland can usefully be distinguished:

1 Coppice

Coppicing is a silvicultural system in which the trees are felled every 5–30 years (depending on the species, their growth rates and the uses of the crops of poles and brushwood) and allowed to grow again mainly from the cut stumps of the previous crop. A few trees, usually oaks, are allowed to grow for sixty or more years as 'standards', which yield building timber. Coppice treatment is known as far back as the Neolithic age and it was the main system in the Middle Ages. Most of our surviving coppice woods are ancient.

2 Wood pasture

This is woodland which is permanently available as pasture. Like coppice, it was a major traditional system of management which developed directly from primitive exploitation of primaeval woodland. Because grazing animals destroy coppice regrowth and inhibit natural regeneration, pasture woods tend to have mainly old trees, many of which were nevertheless cropped by pollarding, i.e. cutting their branches above the reach of animals. Pasture woods took several forms, notably as deer parks and unenclosed woodland on forests and commons. Surviving examples include the ancient oaks of Windsor Great Park and the beech-oak woods of the New Forest. Here ancient woods really do have ancient trees.

3 Highland pine and birch woods

The famous pinewood remnants of the Caledonian forests are a form of ancient wood pasture, which have survived centuries of burning and felling as well as grazing by means of periodic flushes of natural regeneration, rather than by coppicing or pollarding. Many Highland birchwoods have a similar history, but are not so distinctive and are therefore less well known.

4 Woods on inaccessible sites

Woods in Highland ravines and on cliffs or scree are often thought to be almost natural. A famous example is Wistman's Wood, on granite clitter on Dartmoor. In fact, none can have escaped some alteration by man.

5   High forest derived from coppice

In the last 2–300 years some ancient coppices were promoted to high forest, or else oak or beech were planted into the coppice at high density and developed as a dense stand of timber trees in place of the coppice. Examples include the early nineteenth-century oak woods of Alice Holt Forest (Hants) and Dymock Woods (Glos), and the beech woods of the Chilterns.

6   Secondary woods

These are woods which spring up naturally when land is no longer grazed or cultivated. Many modern examples grow on commons where grazing rights are not exercised, and on railway embankments, unploughable slopes and abandoned pits and quarries. Most have been developing for no more than a few decades.

Ancient, semi-natural woods (i.e. most woods in categories 1–5 above) are the most important group for nature conservation. Many are direct descendants of primaeval woodlands which have never been cleared (i.e. primary woodland). Their mixtures of coppice trees and shrubs must be survivals from the original natural woods of Britain. Likewise their soils remain largely undisturbed and can be used as controls in any scientific measurement of the effects of cultivation, etc. on soil properties. Their wildlife communities are usually rich for two main reasons: first, ancient woods tend to have a wider range of habitats than recent woods, and secondly, many woodland species cannot colonise newly-available woodland, or do so slowly over several hundred years. Ancient woods are also historical monuments. As Oliver Rackham (a noted woodland ecologist) would emphasise: since we preserve the battered remains of Bury St Edmunds Abbey, we should also preserve the woods the Abbey once owned at Bradfield, especially as these coppices are intact as in the monks' heyday. Being exceptionally stable features in the landscape, ancient woods contribute enormously to the distinctive and attractive character of certain areas; many of these attributes cannot be recreated once they have been destroyed.

Unfortunately, semi-natural woods are rarely profitable for a timber grower. Most ancient woods have been managed as coppice for

most of the last millenium, yet markets for their products have
declined so far in the last century that this form of treatment has died
out in most areas, and now is only common in parts of Kent.
Admittedly, there is a minor revival of coppicing for fuel, hardwood

Table 2 Fate of ancient, semi-natural woodlands in three areas in the
east Midlands since the early nineteenth century* (hectares)

	Rockingham Forest	Central Lincolnshire	West Cambridgeshire
Total area of ancient woodland in about 1820	7182	3726	700
Remains as woodland in 1972	3558	2558	598
Cleared by 1972	3624	1168	102
Structure and composition of surviving ancient woodland in 1972			
Plantation: Broadleaf	560	326	55
Mixed	523	216	34
Conifer	842	824	56
Felled recently	48	16	21
Parkland	3	7	–
Semi-natural: Traditional coppicing continues	74	2	13
Not traditionally treated; mostly 'derelict' coppice	1493	1167	413
Scrub, mostly thorns	15	–	6
Proportion of early nineteenth century ancient woodland which survived as semi-natural woodland in 1972 (%)	22	31	62
Proportion of the ancient, semi-natural woodland present in 1947 which could still be classified as semi-natural in 1972	56	52	68

*From investigations by Paul Harding and George Peterken

Table 3 Rate of clearance of ancient woodlands (ha per year) in three
areas in the east Midlands*

Period	Rockingham Forest	Central Lincolnshire	West Cambridgeshire
1650–1796	3.9	?	?
1796–c1820	32.7	?	?
c1820–1887	44.9	15.6	0.7
1887–1946	4.7	1.1	0.7
1946–1972	15.9	2.1	9.3
1972–1980	?	4.6	?

*From investigations by Paul Harding and George Peterken

pulp, fencing, etc. but if a landowner wishes to undertake forestry he
is more likely to be advised to fell and plant, an act which destroys the
semi-natural mixture of coppice species. In any case, many ancient
woods are small and surrounded by farmland, so the incentive to
manage them as woods is minimal and the commercial benefits of
clearance to agriculture are overwhelming. Accordingly, there has
been a substantial decline in ancient, semi-natural woods since the
early nineteenth century (see Table 2, p. 67) at rates which have varied
enormously between areas and over different periods (see Table 3).
Probably some 30–60 per cent of all ancient woods present in 1947
have since been cleared or converted to plantation forestry.

Britain still has as much as 300 kha of ancient, semi-natural
woodland. A few woods survive because they are commercially
beneficial to their owners, but most are neglected, used only as
pheasant preserves, or have become nature reserves, amenity woods
or public open spaces. The Nature Conservancy Council had, by
1974, scheduled 124 kha of woodland as sites of special scientific
interest, national nature reserves, forest nature reserves and local
nature reserves. County naturalists' trusts, the National Trust and
county councils have also acquired many woods. The Forestry Commission is statutorily responsible for maintaining the 'Ancient and
Ornamental' woods of the New Forest, and co-operates with other
bodies elsewhere. Many of these arrangements are essentially holding
operations or deferred decisions on future management. If the particular and irreplaceable features of ancient, semi-natural woods are to
survive indefinitely, then the long-term solutions must be either a

return to commercial viability of traditional management or something like it, or secure establishment as a 'conservation' wood in some sense with appropriate low-intensity management.

The future of small woods

Small woods – those less than 10 ha – scattered throughout the agricultural countryside present particular conservation problems. Since costs such as fencing are high in relation to area they are unprofitable for plantation forestry, and in any case they are insignificant in relation to the total farm area. As a result they are mostly neglected in a silvicultural sense, and the conviction has grown that they must therefore be deteriorating and likely to vanish. To some extent this is true. The tiny woods of upland districts in Wales, for example, are regularly grazed by sheep and cattle seeking shelter from adjacent fields and moors. Many woods in the lowlands were dominated by elms which have lately fallen victim to disease. However, none of these factors weighs as heavily as agricultural intensification: between 1946–72, 368 ha of mostly small woods were cleared in central Lincolnshire and west Cambridgeshire, and 339 ha of this was for agriculture.

Small woods may be insignificant for timber production and represent a loss of opportunity for profitable agriculture, but they do provide cover for game and, most importantly, habitat diversity in what would otherwise be monotonous countryside. They are probably more important as features in the landscape than as wildlife habitats, for, like hedges, they are usually stocked only with widespread species. Like hedges also, their fate depends on the will of farmers to keep them and on the way they are treated. If they provide neither sport nor shelter, then perhaps they provide useful timber or fuel for the farm or attractive landscape which the farmer himself enjoys.

Appropriate management depends on the state of the small wood. Those which originated as plantations and are now mature will probably need to be felled and replanted over a period. Those which were coppiced ought to be coppiced again. Those which are grazed will have to be fenced. In many woods natural regeneration will be sufficient to perpetuate the wood, provided that farm stock, rabbits and hares can be kept down – or out – over the critical period. Recognising the problems and the lack of incentives the Forestry Commission has given grants for replanting small woods, but with only limited success. Applications for planting grants are ineligible if restoration requires only a fence or coppicing. Natural regeneration is less generously aided than planting. Full planting grants are obtained only when the wood is virtually clear-felled and densely planted, but this timber-production approach is generally inappropriate. These deficiencies are partly remedied in some counties by help from county councils and the Countryside Commission.

Conservation guidelines for woodland managers

Woodland managers who want to do the right thing for conservation are encouraged to consider the following points. They are no substitute for direct, on-the-spot advice from a specialist, but may help when this is unavailable:

Keep the woods you have. Minimise clearance to agriculture, etc. New woods planted on unwooded ground are no substitute for old woods: the wildlife is not as rich.

Encourage maturity. Retain trees as long as possible. When felling is necessary, keep a scatter of old trees within the new generation. This not only helps save wildlife, – e.g. woodpeckers – but keeps woods visible in the landscape.

Encourage native tree species. They not only support richer wildlife communities, but they also blend better into the landscape. By using only those species which are already present in a wood one may maintain an ancient, semi-natural woodland community.

Encourage diversity within reason. This applies to structure, habitats such as rides, as well as tree and shrub species. Do not, however, introduce monkey puzzle trees into an oakwood just to add to diversity: their place is in an arboretum.

Restock by natural regeneration of coppice regrowth wherever possible. This favours native species and others already present. Natural regeneration is usually irregular, so structural diversity is maintained. If it works you save the cost of planting.

Look after populations of rare and local species. Ask the naturalist to identify and advise on treatment, if any. Glades and rides may have to be kept open to perpetuate grassland species which have been evicted from intensively arable land.

Keep records of management. If you don't at least note what you have done and where you did it, your successors will be unable to evaluate the long-term consequences properly.

Minimise change. An important, indeed fundamental, principle at the heart of both landscape and nature conservation. For example, if you have a mature wood, restock it over a long period so that there are always some mature patches present. If your wood has been coppiced in the past, try to coppice it again. If your wood contains mature conifers, make sure that some are included in new plantings on the same site. If, for whatever reason, you have a patchwork of broadleaf and conifer stands, restrict future conifer plantings to those patches where conifers now grow. Some wildlife species are slow to adjust to change, but these measures may enable them to keep pace. Most landscape objections to forestry are reactions against *rapid* change.

Forestry and conservation

Forestry in the broad sense can claim precedence in conservation, for the medieval Royal forests were a form of habitat conservation, designed to yield continuously both deer and timber. Latterly, however, and despite protestations to the contrary, forestry has narrowed to its official definition embodied in the primary objective of the Forestry Commission, namely to grow utilisable timber as economically as possible. Pursuit of this objective led to clashes with other interests and now, as a result, the Forestry Commission is required and empowered to take greater account of landscape, wildlife, public recreation, etc. Nevertheless, the principal divide between timber growing and other objectives remains.

Clearly a balance must be struck between timber-growing and competing objectives: but how and where? Two approaches have been adopted: segregation of objectives, and modification of forestry practice. Many woods have been set aside as nature reserves or acquired by local authorities and the National Trust as public open spaces. In almost all such cases these woods are managed in such a way as to maintain their contribution to the landscape. In addition, local authorities have placed Tree Preservation Orders on private woods which are important in the landscape and not already committed to timber production through Forestry Commission grant-aid schemes. In all these woods, as well as in numerous game coverts, timber production has been largely, but not entirely disregarded. The second measure, modification of forestry practice, developed in response to criticism of the effects of unrestrained timber production and harvesting. In order to improve the landscape more broadleaves have been planted or retained than might be commercially justified. The shapes of felling and planting areas have been designed to harmonise with the land forms. Fringes of mature woodland have been retained whilst the core has been felled and replanted. The localities of rare species have often been left undisturbed, and shrubs have been allowed to grow along ride margins for the benefit of birds and insects. There has even been talk of admitting sheep and cattle back into maturing upland conifer plantations.

These measures have not been entirely satisfactory. Segregation is a reasonable strategy, but there is no guarantee that, for example, the most natural or wildlife-rich woods will become nature reserves. Modified forestry ensures that no interest is ignored, but equally that no interest prevails where it should. Furthermore, the multiplicity of objectives can be confusing and expensive, and in the future, as pressure for increased timber production grows, agreements made in the past may be rescinded.

Perhaps the most straightforward and eventually satisfactory solution would be to build on the main division between timber production and other objectives by accepting forestry in the narrow sense in most woodlands and developing a clear and coherent 'alternative forestry' for those woods where timber production should not be the principal objective. We already have much of this division in practice. On one hand there are Forestry Commission woods and those privately-owned woods already dedicated to forestry. On the other we have nature reserves, amenity woods, game coverts, woods subject to Tree Preservation Orders and woods still traditionally treated as coppice and wood pasture: virtually none of these is eligible for financial aid from the government, whereas the Forestry Commission and private woods dedicated to forestry are heavily subsidised. Adopting this approach we would then have two categories of forestry, characterised as follows:

1   Forestry

Objective: timber production. Methods: mainly even-aged plantations of fast growing species. State support: subsidy as necessary for Forestry Commission; grant aid for planting by private owners; tax relief for private growers. Area: 1700 kha of existing woodland, plus new afforestation amounting to perhaps another 1700 kha.

This is essentially 'modern' forestry as we know it. The arrangements for State support introduced during 1981 will adequately promote this form of forestry. Only minor concessions would be made to other objectives within plantations, and most of these would not involve expenditure, e.g. leaving stream sides unplanted or sloping plantation blocks to minimise landscape impact. One hopes that present methods of timber production are indefinitely sustainable – if so, forestry is a form of conservation in the broad sense – but the effects of conifers on soils and the spread of pests must be monitored. Ideally, there would be some mechanism which directed forestry away from land which is already highly valued for landscape and wildlife in its present condition.

2 Alternative forestry

Objective: landscape conservation, nature conservation, public access or game preservation. Methods: traditional management such as coppicing and/or strict application of the guidelines listed in the previous section. State support: a scheme based on management grants, not planting grants, combined with co-ordination of existing advice and schemes organised by local authorities, Countryside Commission, Nature Conservancy Council. Area: about 300 kha, most of which is now ancient, semi-natural woodland, i.e. less than 10 per cent of the projected total woodland area.

Possibly as much as one-third of all the woodland which should be in this category is already assigned to 'alternative forestry', e.g. Epping Forest, the unenclosed New Forest Woods, numerous woodland nature reserves, local authority amenity woods, etc. Wherever possible timber would be produced, subject to the over-riding needs of other objectives.

Further reading

A Brooks, *Woodlands*, British Trust for Conservation Volunteers, 1980. (Gives practical guidance on management.)

G F Peterken, *Woodland Conservation and Management*, Chapman and Hall, 1981. (Provides a national review of woodland types and woodland conservation.)

Oliver Rackham, *Hayley Wood*, Cambridge & Isle of Ely Naturalists' Trust, 1975.

Oliver Rackham, *Trees and Woodland in the British Landscape*, Dent, 1976.

Oliver Rackham, *Ancient Woodland*, Arnold, 1980.
(Rackham's three books provide the best accounts of the ecology and history of semi-natural woodland in Britain.

H M Steven and A Carlisle, *The Native Pinewoods of Scotland*, Oliver and Boyd, 1959.

A G Tansley, *The British Islands and their Vegetation*, Cambridge University Press, 1939. (Contains chapters on woodlands.)

The Ecology of Even-Aged Forest Plantations, Institute of Terrestrial Ecology (ITE), 1979. (Gives a wide-ranging introduction to the new upland forests.)

In addition, the Forestry Commission publishes booklets on all aspects of modern forestry; lists of these are available from HMSO. The bibliographies in Rackham (1980) and ITE (1979) also provide copious entries to the long trail through the literature on forestry and woodlands.

6 Wildlife

Richard Fitter

We are fortunate that very few species of wildlife in Britain today are in danger of immediate extinction. This may seem a bold statement when we have just seen the actual extinction of the large blue butterfly as a British species, when at least one vertebrate, the barbel (a freshwater fish) is believed to have become extinct within the past ten years, and when the otter has disappeared over a wide tract of central and southern England since the 1950s. However, compared with other parts of the world, where many animal and plant species are lost every year, we are in not too bad a shape. This is partly because our main phase of wildlife destruction is past. The wolf, the beaver and the great bustard are long gone, and the bulk of our ancient woodlands, fens, heaths and chalk downs have been destroyed during the past 150 years.

But the fact that comparatively few animals and plants are in imminent danger of extinction in Britain within the next five years does not mean that there is not a great danger to many more species before the end of the century. Despite all the efforts of wildlife conservationists, the habitat our wildlife needs, if it is to survive, is still being eroded at an alarming rate. For instance, the Nature Conservancy Council (NCC) has designated some 3800 sites as SSIs (sites of special scientific interest), representing about 5.3 per cent of the total land surface of Great Britain. These are the absolute minimum that must be preserved to ensure a reasonable variety of wildlife at the beginning of the twenty-first century – now, after all, less than twenty years away. Yet some 4 per cent of these sites are being lost each year. If this rate of erosion continues, only about 700 of the existing SSSIs will still be available to wildlife in the first decade of the next century.

So there is plenty for wildlife conservationists to do.

It is important to stress that while it is the imminent extinction of a species that catches the headlines, it is the insidious long-term loss of habitat that has to be stopped. For example, one of our most threatened species today is the greater horseshoe bat, of which a few hundred are believed to survive in south-west England and south Wales. As this bat depends on a comparatively small number of caves and old buildings in which to hibernate, the first thing is to ensure that these are undisturbed and not used for some purpose that will conflict with the needs of the bats – mushroom-growing, for instance, or tourism. One important roost is in an old building that has only just been rescued from demolition because it was about to collapse. Then, like the kite and many other rare breeding birds, it needs to be protected from both the collectors – some museums and private individuals will pay a high price for the skin of a rare bat – and the researchers and ordinary, curious naturalists, who may not realise that inspecting bats at the wrong moment in their life-cycle, when they are hibernating, may have fatal effects. Fortunately, the greater horseshoe bat is now listed as a legally protected species under the Conservation of Wild Creatures and Wild Plants Act, 1975.

Some plants are similarly listed and, if we take a rare orchid – the military orchid – as an example, we find roughly the same needs. To start with, it has only four known sites in Britain (one in Suffolk and three in the Chilterns) fortunately all protected by the local naturalists' trusts. Besides the safeguarding of these sites from devastation by development or ploughing, they need to be managed. For the military orchid, like many rarities, has rather specialised requirements: it needs a fairly open, warm, sunny site, so that on the one hand scrub must be controlled, and on the other the grass must be kept fairly short, either by mowing or by grazing. And this management must be done at the right time of the year so as not to damage the young flowering shoots, or trample on the leaf rosettes of the young plants. Rare orchids have another problem: they often need to be pollinated by special insects. Since we may not know which that insect is and cannot be sure that it will be available at the right time to pollinate a solitary orchid flowering spike, we often have to resort to artificial pollination to ensure that some seed is set. The orchid also, like the bat, has to be protected from human disturbance, from the collector who picks it deliberately for his herbarium, knowing it to be rare; from the visitor who picks it for his posy of wild flowers, not knowing it to be rare; and from those who will actually dig up the tuber and transplant it to their garden. An additional hazard is the photographer, who, in order to photograph a spike at eye level, will lie flat on the ground, crushing smaller spikes or treading on the young rosettes of next year's flowering spikes. Many orchid conservationists regard photographers as the greatest menace of all, as so many have the ambition to photograph all Britain's rare orchids.

Obviously the less widely the location of a rare animal or plant is known, the safer it will be. However, it is hazardous to operate a one-man scheme for protecting any rare animal or plant you may come across. You may not realise all the threats it is subject to, such as imminent ploughing, afforestation or other development. Much better to join one of the county naturalists' trusts, or specialist national organisations, whose role is discussed below, and help them to protect it. Your local knowledge will be invaluable to them.

It is a great advantage to a rare animal or plant to be in a properly guarded nature reserve. Unfortunately, this is to a large extent the public image of all nature reserves: fenced off places where rare animals and plants grow and the public are kept out. Except during the nesting season of birds, and the flowering season of a few conspicuous rare plants, there are very few nature reserves indeed where everybody needs to be kept out. So long as vandalism can be prevented (and near towns this may be a tall order), picnickers can be stopped from lighting fires and leaving litter (nowadays fewer picnickers light fires, but many more leave litter), and the carrying of guns can be effectively prohibited, there is no reason why most nature reserves should not be open to the public at seasons which are not sensitive for rare or uncommon birds or plants. Collecting must also be prohibited, except under permit (this applies mainly to entomologists), and such undesirable activities as motorcycle scrambling and the dumping of industrial waste must obviously be taboo. Reserves where scientific research is in progress may also have to be off-limits for a period, since the sight of the markers needed to delimit experimental areas or transects seems to stimulate an irresistible desire to uproot them. Bearing all this in mind, what you should be able to do in a nature reserve is quietly to enjoy being in the presence of wildlife, making notes about it if you are that way inclined. Sensitive naturalists prefer to go in ones or twos, and so do even less damage than properly conducted parties, who, whatever care they take, are bound to tread on something.

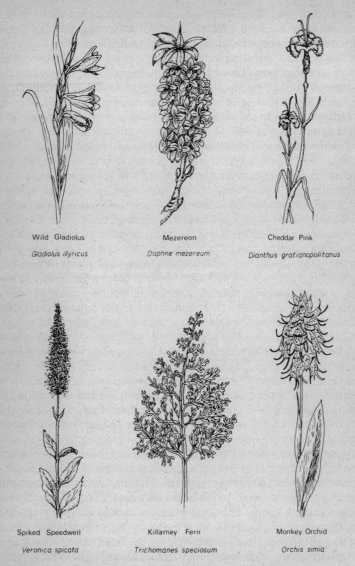

Wild Gladiolus

Gladiolus illyricus

Mezereon

Daphne mezereum

Cheddar Pink

Dianthus gratianopolitanus

Spiked Speedwell

Veronica spicata

Killarney Fern

Trichomanes speciosum

Monkey Orchid

Orchis simia

Figure 12   A selection of plants scheduled for protection (under the Conservation of Wild Creatures and Wild Plants Act 1975)

In addition to their value for preserving rare species, nature reserves have an even greater value in preserving *habitat*. Since destruction of habitat is the major threat to wildlife all over the world, this, rather than the preservation of rare species – important though that is – should be regarded as the main reason for setting up nature reserves. The most threatened habitats in Britain today are wetlands, such as marshes, bogs and fens which are liable to be drained; ancient woodlands of oak, ash, beech and Scots pine, which are liable to be felled and often replanted with non-native conifers such as Japanese larch, Norway spruce and Douglas fir (see Chapter 5); and chalk grasslands which are still being ploughed up, and even when they are not, are liable to degenerate into scrub and ultimately woodland. Any idea that all that is needed after a nature reserve has been acquired is to put a fence around it and leave it alone is now realised to be quite wrong: all nature reserves need to be managed to a greater or lesser degree. Coppice woodland needs to be coppiced at intervals of several years if the bluebells and other spring flowers for which it is famous are not to be shaded out. Chalk grassland must be either grazed or mown, if it is not to revert first to scrub and later to woodland. Wicken Fen, Cambridgeshire (one of Britain's first and most famous nature reserves) has to be managed if the fen is not to dry out and shrubs such as alder buckthorn and sallow are not to supplant the open fen with its interesting rarities and their specialised requirements. In all woodland or scrub reserves the footpaths need to be cut back repeatedly if they are not to grow over. (The extinction of the large blue butterfly itself is a classic example of the need for management. Too late it was discovered that if the butterfly, whose caterpillar spends part of its life cycle in ants' nests, was to thrive, the grass must be kept grazed very short so that its food plant, wild thyme, is not shaded out by tall grasses.)

Nature reserves come in all shapes and sizes, from tiny plots of less than half a hectare to extensive stretches of moorland and mountainside covering several hundred hectares. The smallest nature reserve in Britain is believed to be the Norfolk Naturalists' Trust's Hethel Old Thorn, consisting of a few square metres surrounding this ancient hawthorn tree. The largest is the Beinn Eighe National Nature Reserve in Wester Ross, covering 4252 hectares. They are also of several categories: the Nature Conservancy Council, the main government agency responsible for wildlife conservation, operates a system of 176 national nature reserves, covering 135,000 hectares. By arrangement with the Forestry Commission it also has forest nature reserves, and in conjunction with various local authorities it has scheduled seventy-eight local nature reserves, covering 11,291 hectares.

A much larger number of reserves, though often smaller, is to be found in the voluntary sphere. The largest voluntary body is the Royal Society for the Protection of Birds, with some 300,000 members and eighty reserves covering 36,400 hectares. However, the various county naturalists' trusts, which operate under the umbrella of the Royal Society for Nature Conservation, have between them some 1250 reserves covering over 42,493 hectares.

By no means all reserves are owned by the bodies which run them, and this applies especially to the NCC and the county trusts, which own comparatively few of their reserves – the NCC for example owns only thirty-five – the rest are either leased, or are subject to a more or less formal agreement with the landowner. In addition, quite a number of small reserves are run either by local authorities – for instance, the Oxfordshire County Council has a small educational reserve at Bloxham – or by various natural history societies, such as the Selborne Society, which has an important urban nature reserve at Perivale Wood in Middlesex.

Nature reserves can also be classified according to their purpose. While most national nature reserves are required for scientific research, the aim being to preserve a representative selection of first-class sites largely for this purpose, many local reserves are used as much for amenity as for conserving a particular rare species or threatened habitat. Educational reserves usually contain some habitat, such as oakwood, neutral grassland or scrub, or a flooded gravelpit, which is still sufficiently widespread for it not to matter if it is subjected to a fairly heavy treatment by trampling feet or the collecting of common plants for demonstration purposes. The existence near any large centre of population of one or more educational reserves is of great importance for the future of wildlife conservation.

Most of the more important first- and second-class sites which are worthy of reserve status have been identified in a survey conducted by the NCC and published in 1977 as *A Nature Conservation Review*. There are some 735 such sites, by no means all yet protected, and a few more have been identified since, notably Wendlebury Mead in Oxfordshire, now on its way to becoming a national nature reserve. However, this still leaves the great bulk of the 3800 sites of special scientific interest mentioned earlier to be preserved by county trusts, if they can, and probably many sites that ought to be SSSIs have not yet been identified. The task of safeguarding all these sites, even supposing the various bodies were to succeed in buying, leasing or making agreements for the greater part of them, is immense. It is likely to be many years before any committed wildlife conservationist can complain that there is not enough for him to do.

What can the individual do about nature reserves? One thing is to keep an eye open in your district for good sites in need of preservation, and notify these to your local county trust. Equally, it is important to warn the trust of any threats of development of any kind to such sites. It is always easier to ward off a threat if the site is known and recognised to be of value – so don't wait for the bulldozers before you set off the alarm. By then it is probably too late.

Another good way of helping is to join either the National Conservation Corps, run by the British Trust for Conservation Volunteers from Wallingford, with ten regional offices, or one of the numerous local conservation corps, which the BTCV or your county trust will be able to tell you about. These corps go out every weekend in some part of the country to do various management jobs. Scrub clearance is one of the staples since so much of our grassland, especially on the southern chalk, became overgrown after the myxomatosis epidemic of the 1950s decimated the rabbits which had been preventing it from growing up. But there are many other jobs, such as fencing, clearing out overgrown ponds and weeding young plantations, that have to be done if our growing estate of nature reserves is to be kept in good heart.

The ordinary citizen can also do a great deal to help wildlife, quite apart from the problems of endangered species and nature reserves which occupy all the limelight. Everybody who has a garden can help, both by planting suitable trees and shrubs to help the birds with winter food and by not splashing pesticides about. Do not use long-lasting pesticides, if you can possibly avoid it; those based on pyrethrum, for instance, do not stay in the environment. Apply then as sparingly as possible and only on the actual plants which you need to protect. Later on you may wonder why you do not have more birds in your garden and not realise that it is because you have been soaking their environment with poison, so that the worms and insects they eat are killing them. Before these pesticides were invented people managed without them, and it is still possible to do so if you value wildlife above obsessive tidiness in the garden. If you still feel strongly about seeing aphids on your roses or broad beans, why not try a little biological control? The larvae of ladybirds are among the chief predators of aphids, and are killed, along with the aphids, by spraying. It is certainly worth transplanting any ladybird larvae you may find to aphid-infested, or potentially infested, plants to see if they will do the job for you without resort to a pesticide that will harm the environment for a long time.

The best trees and shrubs to plant to encourage birds into your garden in winter are the berry-bearing ones beloved of thrushes, blackbirds and, in the years when these scarce birds irrupt in Britain, waxwings. Cotoneasters, hawthorns and the genus *Sorbus*, which includes the rowan or mountain ash and the various relatives of our native white beam, should be the staples of any planting for birds. Mezereon berries are also popular with both blackbirds and green-finches. Butterflies, if you like to have them in your garden, natur-ally have quite different requirements. The butterfly bush *Buddleia davidii* will attract large numbers of butterflies, especially small tor-toiseshells, peacocks, red admirals and, in some favoured gardens, even commas, during the buddleia's late summer and early autumn flowering period. Peacocks and small tortoiseshells both have cater-pillars that feed on stinging nettles, so that to encourage them you must leave a few beds of nettles in corners of the garden where they will not offend the tidy-minded. Some people treat plants like stinging nettles as though their very existence in an otherwise cultivated or managed area imply some degree of moral turpitude in the gardener or householder. If you are out to encourage wild creatures of all kinds, which of course includes many insects and other invertebrates, there is great virtue in having a patch of ground where human beings will not venture because they get stung if they do so. So stand up for the stinging nettle, and every small tortoiseshell will bless you!

What applies to domestic gardens also applies, of course, to school gardens. Individual plots may not be able to have berry-bearing shrubs or butterfly bushes, but there must be some corner of the school grounds where these, and stinging nettles too, can be encour-aged.

Zoos and other wildlife collections have a valuable part to play in wildlife conservation, especially in educating the public. It is no good expecting people to want to save wildlife if they do not know what it looks like. And while TV is an effective means of showing animals and plants to millions of people, there is no substitute for the sight of a live animal or plant. So one of the prime justifications for keeping animals in captivity is that it strengthens the desire in many people that the animals they see should be allowed to go on living in their own habitats in the wild. Increasing numbers of zoos are breeding their own animals, and this is as it should be, for it is by no means certain that in twenty years' time they will be able to continue drawing on the wild for their stocks, especially of such animals as the rhinoceros, hippopotamus, elephant, lion and tiger. Lions breed very well in captivity, but with many other animals, zoo keepers have not yet got the right techniques to encourage them to breed. There is a specially important reason to encourage captive breeding of endangered species, for there is always the hope that the species may be re-established in the wild from captive-bred stocks. This has already happened with the nene or Hawaiian goose; birds reared by Sir Peter Scott's Wildfowl Trust at Slimbridge on the Severn Estuary have been released again on the island of Maui in Hawaii, and appear to be re-establishing themselves. The same is also about to happen with that attractive antelope, the Arabian oryx; animals reared in captivity at Phoenix and San Diego Zoos in the United States, as the result of the Fauna and Flora Preservation Society's Operation Oryx in 1962, have recently been returned to both Jordan and Oman. In Oman they will soon be released into the desert, and protected from poachers – who appear to have exterminated the wild oryx – by members of the Harassis tribe who will act as guardians.

What applies to zoos applies of course also to botanic gardens. They have a most valuable educational as well as scientific function, and are increasingly being used as genetic banks for endangered species. These genetic banks are a collection of plants which can be propagated by seeds or cuttings, thus ensuring the survival of rare species. So far, however, we do not have a case of an extinct or endangered plant that has been grown in a botanic garden being re-established in the wild, although several plants believed to be extinct in the wild have recently been found still growing in botanic gardens.

In conclusion, I would like to repeat that it is *habitat* which is all-important for the survival of wildlife. It is no good breeding animals or plants in captivity if their natural habitat is lost. The laws of evolution steadily change the genetic make-up of animals and plants kept away from their natural habitat and they begin to adapt to life in captivity. The Wildlife and Countryside Act 1981 may help to stem the tidal wave of habitat destruction at present going on in Britain, but many conservationists fear that it will prove to be a 'toothless tiger'.

Further reading

Richard Fitter, *Wildlife in Britain*, Penguin, 1963. Although out of print, this book provides a good general introduction to the subject.

Richard Mabey, *The Common Ground*, Hutchinson, 1980. An excellent book providing an overall view of nature conservation in Britain, with particular reference to the work of government bodies.

F H Perring and L Farrell, *British Red Data Books I: Vascular Plants*, Society for the Promotion of Nature Conservation, 1977. The standard book on endangered plants in Britain.

Derek Ratcliffe (ed.), *A Nature Conservation Review*, 2 vols, Cambridge University Press, 1977. These reference books provide much information on specific sites and nature reserves.

Marion Shoard, *The Theft of the Countryside*, Temple Smith, 1980. This controversial book sets out the case for nature conservation against agriculture, and attempts to provide solutions to the problems.

Tony Soper, *The Bird Table Book*, David and Charles, 1965. Practical advice for those wishing to look after birds in the garden.

7 Energy

Hugh Miall

The world energy situation

Most of the energy the world consumes is in the form of fossil fuels – coal, oil and natural gas. The origin of these fuels dates back to the Carboniferous Era and before, 350 million years ago. Deposits of dead vegetation and animal matter were laid down and compressed by geological forces over millions of years. These fossil fuels are now being extracted from the earth at a rate equivalent to 8600 million tonnes of coal a year. Because they are a non-renewable resource, the age of dependence on fossil fuels is bound to be brief in historical time (see Fig. 13).

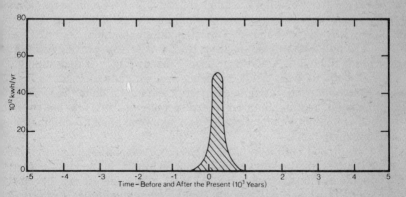

Figure 13   World fossil fuel consumption

In a shorter timescale, the world has large reserves of coal, enough to last 300 years if present consumption trends continue. But the readily available supplies of oil and natural gas, which meet 70 per cent of the energy needs of most industrialised countries, could be exhausted within thirty years (see Fig. 14).

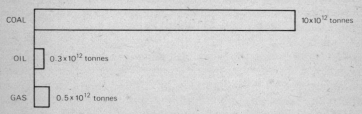

Figure 14 Estimated world fossil fuel resources

Within this period, the world will have to adjust from increasing oil supplies at a current rate of 5 per cent p.a. to a period in which oil supplies will actually be declining. The extraction of oil is expected to peak in 1990; after that a decline is predicted, since the rate of discovery of new oilfields is failing to keep pace with the reduction in output from existing fields.

Oil will not run out physically, it will simply become too expensive to extract economically. As wells are exhausted, interest will turn to the vast deposits of oil trapped in tar sands and oil shales, and to oil left in wells that have already been tapped (in the past only a quarter of the oil in the average well was extracted). But it is difficult and expensive to recover oil from such sources; mining the tar sands and the oil shales will also have a severe impact on the environment.

The situation with natural gas is similar. The main existing fields in Europe and North America are near or already past their peak supply. And while new gas fields are being brought on stream in Alaska, Siberia, the Arctic, Algeria and Iran, these are far from the world's population centres. In order to exploit these fields the gas has to be transported through long pipelines or shipped as liquefied natural gas in tankers.

The prospect of future scarcity has precipitated a sharp increase in fuel prices, and the West's dependence on Middle East oil has created dangerous international tensions. Well before the oil and gas are physically exhausted, the political and economic effects of the energy crisis are already upon us.

How energy is used in the UK

With its large coal reserves and its North Sea oil and gas, the United Kingdom is more favourably placed than many industrialised countries. But in its pattern of energy demand, the British economy is as heavily dependent on oil and natural gas as other industrialised countries. We face a formidable transition over the next thirty years as these fuels become less available and more expensive.

It is useful to distinguish between three levels at which energy is used. 'Primary energy' is the total national supply of energy from all sources. Fig. 15a shows the share of different energy sources in meeting primary energy demand. 'Delivered energy' is energy supplied to consumers and excludes conversion losses in the energy supply industries. Fig. 15b shows the share of different fuels in delivered energy. This gives a more accurate picture of the pattern of energy use by consumers than the primary energy breakdown. Fig. 15c shows the 'end-uses', or purposes, for which energy is consumed.

From Fig. 15c one can see that 66 per cent of delivered energy is used to provide heat for buildings and industrial processes. A further 26 per cent is used for transport fuels and only 8 per cent is for electricity-specific uses, such as lighting, electric appliances, electric motors and electrolysis. Thus 92 per cent of energy consumed is required for heat or transport, the overwhelming bulk of which at present comes from oil and natural gas. Our immediate problem, therefore, is to provide for heating and transport needs when oil and natural gas supplies begin to decline. The way in which energy is supplied and used in this country is also illustrated by an energy flow chart (Fig. 16).

Nuclear power is often claimed to be a substitute for the fossil fuels, but on careful examination it seems unlikely to fulfil this claim. At present nuclear power provides 14 per cent of Britain's electricity. However, electricity is only 12 per cent of delivered energy, so the nuclear contribution to delivered energy needs is only 14 per cent of 12 per cent – about 2 per cent (Fig. 15b). In 1980 there were fourteen nuclear power stations, and the government intends building one more each year from 1982 to the end of the century. Even then, on the projected growth in electricity demand, nuclear energy would supply little more than 20 per cent of electricity supply (4 per cent of delivered energy). As it stands, the nuclear programme will increase the share of nuclear power in the electricity part of the pie (Fig. 15b),

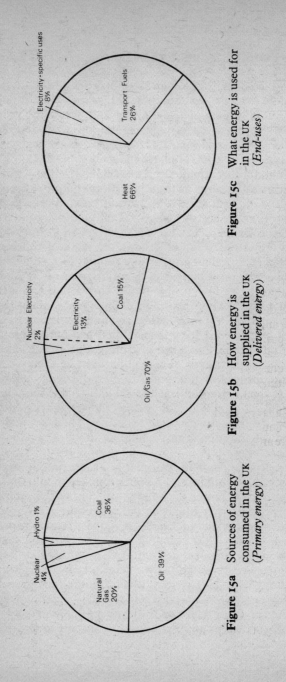

Figure 15a Sources of energy consumed in the UK (*Primary energy*)

Coal 36%
Hydro 1%
Nuclear 4%
Natural Gas 20%
Oil 39%

Figure 15b How energy is supplied in the UK (*Delivered energy*)

Nuclear Electricity 2%
Electricity 13%
Coal 15%
Oil/Gas 70%

Figure 15c What energy is used for in the UK (*End-uses*)

Electricity-specific uses 8%
Transport Fuels 26%
Heat 66%

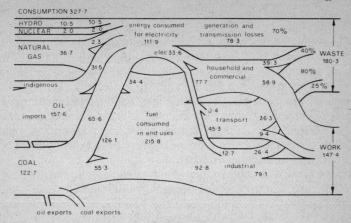

Figure 16 Energy flow in the UK

but will do nothing to substitute for oil and natural gas in their role as heating and transport fuels. The main fuel used to generate electricity now is coal, so increasing nuclear power will mainly displace coal, not oil and gas. Since nuclear power provides only electricity, it cannot substitute for oil as a liquid fuel, nor can it economically replace gas for heating. Only if most vehicles were electric and most buildings were electrically heated could nuclear power substitute for oil and gas on a large scale. This would mean building hundreds of nuclear power stations, many of them necessarily near towns.

There are plentiful supplies of coal, which could be used to produce synthetic liquid fuel and substitute natural gas. At the moment these are extremely expensive to produce, but as fuel prices rise they may become competitive, and pilot conversion plants are being built in Australia, Germany and the USA and are already in operation in South Africa. Synthetic fuel plants have environmental problems, however; they are giant industrial facilities, physically similar to oil refineries, and require vast quantities of water and emit considerable air and water pollution.

More coal could also be burnt directly in industry and in domestic heating. But if the national consumption of coal is increased, more pits will have to be opened, some in areas which have not been mined before. The protracted public inquiry following the National Coal Board's 1979 application to open mines in the Vale of Belvoir, a historic and scenic rural area, showed that plans to expand mining will meet with vigorous local resistance.

On a global scale, if the world consumption of coal continues to increase, there is likely to be a rise in the concentration of CO_2 in the earth's atmosphere. This has increased from 265–90 parts per million in 1850 to 330 parts per million in 1978. If the CO_2 level were to rise to double its pre-industrial level, some fear that the atmosphere's average temperature could rise by 1°C, which could change the earth's climate sufficiently to disrupt human agriculture and alter the habitats of many species. Coal thus represents a very substantial resource but one with very substantial drawbacks.

Many of the renewable sources of energy can provide heat directly – notably solar and geothermal. Organic wastes and specially grown crops ('biomass'), could contribute to liquid fuel requirements. Such technologies are available today but will take time to come into general use. It is a matter of controversy how much energy they could supply without making excessive claims on land and other resources. In principle the renewable sources are capable of supplying several times the energy currently consumed in the UK, but in practice their contribution will be limited to much less than this.

The first priority in tackling Britain's dependence on oil and natural gas must be to ensure that these fuels are used efficiently. Fortunately the scope for conservation is very great. If present techniques for improving energy efficiency were put into practice throughout the country, the same standard of living and of economic activity could be maintained with less than half the present consumption of primary energy, according to *A Low Energy Strategy for the UK*. A vigorous policy of energy conservation could mean that existing reserves of oil and gas are stretched well into the next century, and possibly beyond.

Energy conservation in buildings

About 55 per cent of Britain's primary energy is used to heat buildings. Modern building practices were developed at a time when energy was cheap and plentiful, and most buildings are very inefficient users of energy. In order to maintain the desired level of comfort in a house, the amount of heat going into the building must equal the amount of heat flowing out. Some heat is lost through ventilation but most of the heat loss is through the fabric of the building. If houses are photographed in winter in the infra-red, the roof, walls, windows and doors can be seen glowing with heat. The amount of heat lost in this way depends on the insulating qualities of the building's fabric. Heat losses also vary from one building to another, depending on the size, shape, exposure to wind and the materials used. A typical uninsulated semi-detached house loses 25 per cent of its heat through the roof, 35 per cent through the walls, 15 per cent through the floor, 10 per cent through windows and 15 per cent in ventilation losses.

Fabric losses can be cut by more than 50 per cent with insulation and double-glazing. It is cost-effective to put at least 100mm of insulation in the loft and to fill cavity walls with insulating foam. Solid walls can be insulated either internally or externally, and suspended timber floors insulated from beneath. Multiple glazing, heavy curtains and night shutters can make dramatic savings in losses through windows. Other worthwhile measures included lagging the hot water tank and hot water pipes and checking, and if necessary modifying, thermostat and radiator controls. Draughtstripping on internal doors and curtains over staircases can reduce the flow of heat from downstairs to little-used upstairs rooms. Ventilation losses occur through heated air flowing out of the building through doors, windows, gaps around doors and window frames, and leaks through floorboards, ceiling, brickwork, etc. In most houses in Britain the rate of ventilation is so high that all of the air in the house is replaced completely every half hour. Simple measures like weatherstripping doors and windows and blocking sources of draughts can reduce ventilation losses by half. When these simple measures are complete, it is possible to make further improvements by installing mechanical ventilation systems with heat recuperators to recover heat from the exhaust air. These can reduce ventilation losses by over 75 per cent.

Once the house is thoroughly insulated and draughtproofed, the efficiency of the heating system can be improved. An open coal fire for example has a thermal efficiency of only 5–30 per cent, whereas the most modern gas and coal boilers have efficiencies of 70 or 80 per cent. Electric heaters are 100 per cent efficient at the point of use, but only 30 per cent efficient if losses in the power station and the national grid are taken into account (two-thirds of the heat generated in the power station is wasted due to the low thermal efficiency of converting fuel to electricity). Highly efficient heat pumps can draw heat out of cold air and use only one unit of electricity to produce up to three units of heat.

These energy efficiency improvements make it possible to maintain a given temperature in the house with a lower use of energy. Energy can be saved more directly by reducing internal temperatures. Every 1°C rise in temperature over 18°C requires a 10 per cent increase in energy consumption for space heating. So, lowering the thermostat can make big savings if the house is already too hot. It is certainly quicker and cheaper to insulate yourself by putting on additional clothing than to insulate the whole house!

New houses offer an even greater scope for energy saving. For example, the Wates low energy house at the National Centre for Alternative Technology at Machynlleth, which has 450mm deep insulated walls and quadruple glazing, uses thirteen times less heat than an equivalent conventional house. Indeed, 'superinsulated' houses have been built in Sweden and Canada which require no heating at all, even when it is freezing outside. They get all their heat from solar gain through the windows and 'free heat gains' from lights, cookers, electrical appliances and people's bodies. The house of the future may be a highly insulated structure with large south-facing windows and a high thermal mass, such that the whole house is effectively a solar collector and heat store.

Appliances and lighting

Cookers, refrigerators, freezers and washing machines consume the lion's share of electricity used by domestic appliances. All four machines can be made twice as efficient by added insulation, better controls and improved design. 'Low energy' lights which are on the market consume a third of the electricity of a standard light but give the same amount of illumination. Although energy-efficient appliances may be more expensive to purchase than conventional products, the extra costs are more than paid off in savings on electricity bills.

Vehicles

A typical West European car consumes about 350 gallons of petrol a year, equivalent to about nine barrels of oil. Transport as a whole accounts for 30 per cent of the oil consumed in Western Europe, 50 per cent in the UK and 60 per cent in the USA. The heavy dependence of Western nations on Middle East oil, and the implications of this for international peace, make energy conservation in the transport sector a matter of priority.

In recent years there has been growing interest in the fuel efficiency of cars and other vehicles. Manufacturers are introducing new cars with petrol consumption 75 per cent or less than their predecessors. Even larger savings are technically possible and economically justifiable. Improving fuel efficiency is estimated to add 9 per cent to the cost of a new car. However, if this extra cost is spread over the average lifetime and mileage of the car, the improved efficiency saves energy for 20 per cent of the cost of petrol.

Of course, you can save even more oil if you cycle or walk instead of driving. A vigorous shift towards cycling short distances could save at least 10 per cent of oil used in transport. Public transport is also 2–3 times more fuel-efficient per passenger-mile than private cars.

Industry

About 40 per cent of Britain's primary energy is consumed by industry. The energy intensive industries (iron and steel, metals, glass, bricks, cement, chemicals) consume half of the energy in this sector, although they contribute only 20 per cent of industrial output. The energy consumed per unit of output has been steadily falling as technical progress is made, but there is scope for much more improvement. The best Japanese and Swedish steel mills use 50 per cent of the energy of their UK equivalents, for example. Less energy-intensive industries, for whom energy costs are not a very significant factor in total costs, pay little attention to energy conservation and are generally less efficient in their use of energy than the energy-intensive industries.

Energy can be saved in industry by recovering waste heat which is discharged into the environment, using boilers to generate both heat and electricity, improving controls, reallocating fuels, and making improvements in processes and equipment. At least 25 per cent, and generally 50 per cent, of the energy consumed per unit output can be saved by technical improvements in efficiency. Improving the efficiency of electric motors and replacing some of them by hydraulic motors could save all the electricity that nuclear power now supplies. Dramatic savings in oil can also be made by high-efficiency boilers and by the use of coal-fired equipment where practical.

The Department of Industry has published a number of useful

studies of the scope for reducing energy in specific industries (*The 'Thrift' Reports*), and audits are available free of charge for firms to analyse their energy consumption.

Combined heat and power (CHP) and cogeneration

As much as a fifth of the country's primary energy is lost as waste heat in the cooling towers of power stations. This waste heat can be used to heat houses and other buildings if power stations are converted to Combined Heat and Power (CHP). This calls for a mains hot water supply linking the power station to the central heating systems in houses. Whereas the efficiency of a conventional power station is about 34 per cent, a CHP station converts fuel into heat and electricity with an efficiency of 80 per cent, so on a national scale the potential energy savings are substantial. Sweden, Denmark, Russia and Finland have CHP in many of their towns, and a recent Department of Energy report has recommended that CHP should be introduced in large cities in Britain.

CHP is a method which makes efficient use of the heat generated as a by-product of electricity production. It is also possible to generate electricity from boilers at present used only for heat. This is 'cogeneration'. If industrial boilers were used to generate electricity for the national grid, it would save building several new power stations and would give further energy savings. Industry could also generate more of its own electricity needs using this method.

The renewable energy sources

In the long term, we shall have to switch from fossil fuels to sustainable energy sources. Hence the importance of the renewable sources of energy: solar, geothermal, wind, wave, hydro, tidal and biomass. The attraction of these sources is that they are natural energy flows, constantly replenished, and the technologies that tap them are relatively benign in their environmental effects. Their disadvantage is that they are diffuse sources of energy, and a large area of solar collectors, or a large number of windmills, would be required to collect energy on the scale at which is is consumed at present. Most of them are also intermittent sources, and their fluctuations take no account of the rhythms of human life. This makes it necessary to use solar or wind energy in conjunction with fossil fuels as a back-up supply, or with storage facilities capable of storing heat over a daily and seasonal cycle. A promising way of using solar energy is to link a number of solar collectors on a group of houses to a large well-insulated central heat store, capable of storing excess heat collected in summer and delivered in winter. This concept is being developed in Sweden. There is in principle enough roof space on the houses in Britain to meet all of the country's heating needs in this way – assuming that the houses are first insulated to a high standard.

Britain is relatively rich in renewable energy sources. The potential for hydro, wind, tidal and wave energy is very large, and together they could supply more electricity than is generated now. Wind energy is especially promising and can be used either with battery storage or heat pumps and heat storage on a local scale, or it could contribute to the national grid. In 1980 the Central Electricity Generating Board announced plans to construct several large wind turbines.

Geothermal energy is heat from the earth's core. A tenth of the population of Britain lives in areas where it may be possible to recover heat from seven miles below the earth's surface and pipe it through hot water mains to heat houses.

Waste products are another, often neglected, potential source of energy. Agriculture could become energy self-sufficient by converting its wastes into methane and liquid fuels. Urban rubbish can be made into pellets and used in boilers or CHP plants. This would avoid the present practice of dumping rubbish in landfills and could save 2 per cent of primary energy consumption.

However, the renewable sources of energy are most unlikely to contribute as much energy as is consumed now in Britain, without making excessive claims on space. But if buildings, vehicles and industry were first made energy-efficient, and if other resources were also used less wastefully, a society based on sustainable sources of energy would be entirely possible.

What you can do

It is important first to become aware of how wasteful our energy habits are today. The Open University, Milton Keynes, Bucks has a course, *Energy in the Home*, which gives instructions for monitoring domestic energy consumption, and there are a number of books available which offer detailed practical advice (see books by Campbell and Hammond listed below). It is well worth visiting the National Centre for Alternative Technology (Llyngwern Quarry, Machynlleth, Powys) where a number of renewable energy and energy conservation technologies are on display. The Centre also offers courses on energy conservation.

Grants for loft insulation are available from local authorities and there are special additional grants for people on social security. As yet, there are no government incentives for other insulation measures, but thorough insulation and weather-stripping are highly cost-effective. It is worth taking out a loan to pay for them if necessary – the repayments will be less than the avoided fuel bills.

For schools, hospitals, commercial and industrial premises, there are Department of the Environment or Department of Industry grants to cover the cost of an energy audit. The audit shows how energy is used in a building and where there is scope for conservation. Professional advice and services on energy conservation are available from a large number of companies; a classified guide to them is available from the Royal Institute of British Architects (see Further Reading).

In some towns (notably Newcastle, Birmingham, Cambridge and Durham) groups like Friends of the Earth or the Newcastle Energy Advice Centre have insulated houses free, using insulation materials given by the council and labour provided by volunteers or people on Job Creation schemes. These local initiatives are models for ways in which all our houses could quickly be brought up to acceptable insulation standards. Local authorities are in a particularly good position to take initiatives on energy conservation (e.g. CHP, fuel from urban waste, insulation of council houses and public buildings) and they should be urged to do so.

Energy conservation is likely to be a growing field in the future, with job opportunities for architects, builders, scientists, engineers, planners and many others with a variety of skills.

Further reading

Peter Campbell, *Beginner's Guide to Home Energy Saving*, Newnes Technical Books, 1979. A clear guide showing how to insulate your house.

Peter Chapman, *Fuel's Paradise*, Pelican, 1979. This book shows how fuels are actually used in Britain and how to calculate energy demands according to different lifestyles.

Department of Energy, Energy Paper 35, *Report of the Working Party on Combined Heat and Power*, HMSO, 1979.

Michael Flood, *Solar Prospects*, Friends of the Earth, 1980. An explanation of renewable energy technologies and what scope there is for them in Britain.

Gerald Foley, *The Energy Question*, Pelican, 1980. The second edition of this excellent discussion of world energy resources.

Garry Hammond et al, *The Energy Consumer's Handbook*, Pan, 1980. A clear introduction to the potential for saving energy, concentrating on household consumption.

Gerald Leach, *A Low Energy Strategy for the UK*, IIED/Science Reviews, 1979. A scenario of energy supply and demand for the next fifty years, including a comprehensive assessment of the scope for conservation in each sector of the economy.

Amory Lovins, *Soft Energy Paths*, Pelican, 1977. The case for a non-nuclear, decentralised energy future.

Energy Conservation Handbook, Royal Institute of British Architects, 1980. Classified guide to energy conservation advice and services.

8 Transport

Nick Lester

Mechanised transport – and in particular the petrol-consuming road vehicle – must be the most immediate environmental problem we face. It affects us all and it affects us now. But it is surely also the most disregarded environmental problem and for the same reasons. Few people consider that very much can be done about it.

Undoubtedly the biggest impact is made by cars and lorries. Motor vehicles use 78 per cent of all energy used in transport, and 18 per cent of all energy used in Britain – this includes 40 per cent of the oil we use. Traffic is widely recognised as the biggest single noise nuisance – a transport and road research laboratory estimate is that 61 per cent of the urban population suffers from unacceptable noise levels, mainly from traffic. Road accidents account for more than seventeen deaths every day, and 335,000 casualties a year – figures that seem to go almost unnoticed. After diseases, road accidents are the biggest single cause of death in Britain. Motor vehicles account for 89 per cent of the 8.7 million tonnes carbon-monoxide pumped into the atmosphere annually, 40 per cent of the 1.3 million tonnes of hydrocarbons and 25 per cent of the 2 million tonnes of nitrogen oxides, as well as 41,000 tonnes of sulphur dioxide, 64,000 tonnes of particulates (smoke, soot and grit) and 7,500 tonnes of lead. And roads alone (i.e. excluding car parks, garages and the like) cover 2,500 square kilometres – an area about the size of Cheshire or Nottinghamshire, while in London, roads constitute as much as 12 per cent of the total area. Lorries in particular, can cause considerable damage to these roads, to the services such as sewers, gas and water mains underneath them and to buildings alongside them – both through vibration and direct hits.

It's not just cars and lorries which cause environmental problems, however. People who live near airports suffer from terrible noise pollution. Nearly 75,000 people suffer unacceptably high levels of noise from the three main airports around London alone, and nearly 1.7 million suffer annoyance. Some people living alongside railways suffer from vibration. But these environmental problems tend to be discounted because so many people see them as inevitable or even necessary, and, of course, nearly everybody contributes by travelling. The scale of the problem has grown with the development in traffic and transport over the last 150 years. But what is often not realised is how much the improvement of transport – making it cheaper, quicker and more comfortable – has directly made the problems larger. Certainly the two implied government policies on transport over the last thirty years – universal car ownership, and the idea that a free market can decide transport provision – have accelerated the process. To see how this has worked we must look at how transport has affected our life styles. A clear example is in the growth of towns and cities in which the provision of transport has played a major, if not a dominating, role.

In the past, the size of a town was limited by the amount of food that could be brought in and distributed or stored according to the daily needs of the inhabitants. The Industrial Revolution and consequent urbanisation increased town sizes, but it was not until the railway and canal systems were developed that cities could expand significantly as food supply ceased to be such a major problem. Towns and cities could now grow quickly. New factories, relying on cheap transport of raw materials, sprang up at rail heads and along waterways and the workers clustered closely round them. Later in the nineteenth century the more wealthy began to leave the city centres to live in the country – the railways enabled them to live further out but still get to work each day. Commuting was born and the suburbs started to be built.

Sir Arthur Conan-Doyle, in a *Sherlock Holmes* story, refers to a drive through the *rural areas* between central London and the 'village' of Lee. Only seven miles from the centre of London, the coming of the railway had enabled city clerks to move out into the 'country' transforming Lee into an inner-London suburb (a part of Lewisham), which it still is today.

Property developers were not slow to take advantage of this trend. And often the railway companies, then privately owned, themselves encouraged these property developments as they increased their

Table 4 Energy consumption by UK Modes of Transport

Method of transport		Energy efficiency by mode of transport			Energy used in 1978 (million therms)
		Freight (tonne-km/gallon)	Assumed passenger load*	Passengers (pass-km/gallon)	
Air	Airbus	6–12	55%	75	2,005
Rail	Inter-City		45%	158	505
	Commuter		25%	144	
	Bulk freight	132–395			
	General goods	93–316			
Car	Motorway/rural		2	96	
	Local/urban		1½	51	
Lorry	Bulk freight	66–113			10,300 approx.
	General goods	45–176			
Coach			65%	395	400 approx.
Bus			25%	198	
Waterway		400			518
Pipeline		480			10 approx.

Notes
*The percentage capacity assumed to be occupied.

Air figures from *Energy in Transport* (Transport 2000, 1974); waterways and pipelines estimates updated from earlier tonne-miles/gallon figures; other estimates of energy efficiency from Department of Energy Papers nos. 10 and 24.

The estimates of energy used are on a heat supplied basis, from *Transport Statistics 1968–78*, Table 165, with approximations for coach/bus and pipeline.

passenger traffic. The Metropolitan railway in particular, is associated with this practice, having developed Metroland, an area covering 200 sq km. Development of the railways was followed by that of the trams and buses and was responsible for the great suburban sprawls of the first forty years of this century.

The same pattern is even more true of the car. Instead of living in fairly dense developments – typically up to ten minutes' walk from the bus stop or railway station – ten minutes' drive has become the rule for many. Cheaper cars and petrol in real terms as a percentage of earnings leading to rapidly increasing car ownership in the thirty years following the Second World War has immeasurably strengthened the push of the cities into the country. The only thing to hold back this process was the traffic congestion in the towns which discouraged people from driving to work. But the vast urban road-building programmes of the 1960s and 1970s, while not solving the problem, did allow more drivers to take part. As new roads opened so more people transferred from public to private transport, taking advantage of easier driving – at least temporarily.

This has had two effects. First, public transport has suffered from a very familiar – and vicious – spiral of decline: fewer passengers leads to less revenue for the companies, which then reduce services which leads in turn to even fewer passengers. Secondly, as people have moved into the country, so they have to travel further for their everyday facilities. Instead of the local shop or pub being only a short walk around the corner, it's now a drive away. And once you're in the car it's just as easy to drive a little further still.

This has led to the closing of many local shops, schools, pubs and libraries – the list seems endless. This is all very well for those who do own cars, but is an absolute disaster for those who don't. They are forced to rely on a poor, but expensive, bus or train service for even the smallest needs.

The scant attention given by both central and local government to solving the problems of car ownership and related problems, such as congestion and lack of parking facilities has not helped either. What is surprising is that car drivers and car journeys are still surprisingly relatively few. As Fig. 17 shows, there are almost as many journeys made on foot as by car – about 40 per cent – and the number of trips made by public transport is equally significant.

So what can be done to make the picture brighter? Undoubtedly, our main emphasis must be to get more support for, and more people

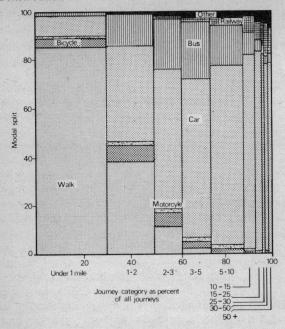

Figure 17   Percentage of journeys of different lengths by
different modes

on to public transport. Environmentally, the advantages of public
over private transport are very clear. Buses and trains are all far more
efficient in their use of energy than cars. (While bicycles and feet
require no fossil fuel energy at all!)

In land use terms too, public transport is absolutely paramount. A
standard 7.3 metre wide road can carry a maximum of 17,000 cars per
(16 hours) day; that is a little more than 1,000 cars per hour. At a
maximum this could represent some 5,000 people per hour, although
at peak hours the average car occupancy rate is only about 1.2 people
per car, which equates to some 1,500 people per hour. By contrast one
can see that the same number of buses could carry up to 40,000 people
per hour, and a double-track railway line as many as 72,000 people per
hour. In addition one should allow for the fact that people can get off
or on a train much quicker than a bus or car, because there are so many
more doors, thus a railway is even more efficient in land use terms.

And this does not even include the space taken up by car parking. According to *The Bicycle Planning Book*, car passengers, who make up 11.4 per cent of the people entering central London at peak hours, take up 87 per cent of the space, whereas public transport passengers, who make up 63 per cent, take up no more than 7 per cent of the space.

In terms of pollution the public transport user also scores over the car user. Properly maintained diesel engines (which power buses and diesel trains, electric trains being even cleaner) emit comparatively little in the way of pollution, whereas petrol engines emit carbon monoxide, nitrogen oxides and lead. Lead is increasingly recognised as a major environmental poison. Always recognised as poisonous if taken in large amounts, lead is now being more widely identified as a cause of mental impairment in children if taken in small quantities. Despite the recent government report by the Lawther Committee which minimised this problem steps have now been taken by the government to reduce lead level from 0.40 to 0.15 g per litre in the lead emitted by vehicles by 1985.

In safety terms, too, public transport has a more impressive record than private transport. Of the 6,350 people killed on the roads in 1979 only thirty-one were bus passengers. That gives an accident rate of 0.1 deaths per 100 million passenger/kilometres for buses, and twenty accidents of all severities per 100 million passenger/kilometres. The accident rate for cars is 0.7 deaths per 100 million passenger/kilometres and thirty-seven accidents. This means that, mile for mile, it is seven times more likely that you will be killed and nearly twice as likely that you will be involved in an accident travelling by car than by bus. Travelling by train is safer still, with only eight people killed in railway accidents in 1979, and only 354 passengers injured. This gives an accident rate of 0.1 deaths per million passenger/kilometres and thirteen accidents.

It is therefore clear that it is environmentally desirable to promote public transport. But there are two further reasons why it cannot be dispensed with. First, there will always be people who are not able to own a car – the young, the poor and people who simply do not have the capability to drive. In addition, in households which do own a car, only one person can drive at once, so anyone who wants to go somewhere different from the driver has to use other means of transport.

Second, given the space that a car takes up, even if all cars carried

the maximum number of passengers (instead of the average occupancy of 1.6 as at present) it would still be physically impossible to
squeeze enough cars into major cities without major reconstruction. A
city like London, for example, is already congested most of the day,
and extremely congested at peak hours – and this with only a minority
of journeys made by car. It is estimated that it would be necessary to
increase road space *six-fold* to cater for cars if all commuters used
them. Given that road space already takes about 20 per cent of
London's total area (if all parking and service facilities are included),
this is clearly impossible.

Having accepted the idea, then, that some public transport is
necessary, it is far more sensible to support and provide public
transport which runs full rather than empty. Thus there is an
economic as well as environmental case for supporting public transport. How you achieve this is another question, but experience shows
that two elements are necessary. First, there must be attractions to
draw people out of their cars, and second, there must be a stick to
drive them out. Either strategy on its own will not be successful.

Attracting people on to public transport can only be achieved by
giving a good service with low fares. This undoubtedly costs money,
but will probably be cheaper than large road building schemes that
may otherwise be necessary. South Yorkshire County Council and
Lothian Regional Council have adopted this policy. In both cases,
fares are low – South Yorkshire last had a fares rise in 1975 – and the
number of passengers using the buses continues to increase. Bus
priority measures, special bus lanes, bus streets, and access to pedestrianised areas are also needed.

The other side of the coin is traffic management and restraint. The
main objective must be to cater for the people who live in the city
rather than the cars passing through it. This will entail parking
control: closing up back streets – currently used by cars as 'rat-runs' –
in order to let children play there safely; pedestrianised shopping
centres; and only providing car parking on the outskirts in conjunction with park-and-ride schemes to the city centre, making it more
difficult for motorists to drive *through* town centres.

The reason why restraint is needed as well as better public transport
is because of the way most drivers perceive travelling by car. Most
think that travelling into town is quicker by car, but tend to ignore the
time spent driving around looking for a parking space. Most think it is
also cheaper, thinking only of the petrol costs (ignoring wear and tear,

oil consumption etc.), and some drivers don't even consider the price of petrol if they don't have to fill up on the way. In fact, public transport is almost always cheaper when there are less than three people in the car if you include *all* the car's costs. There is also the in-built aversion to change to be overcome.

As mentioned earlier, in general terms neither central nor local government has supported public transport in the past. Instead they have supported increased car use and the necessary increased road building for the past twenty-five years. Anyone opposing this policy used to be ruthlessly disregarded. It was this contemptuous regard for others' points of view that, in itself led to the first serious challenges to the accepted wisdom which took the form of disrupted motorway inquiries in the early 1970s.

Before 1970, new roads were almost universally welcomed. They provided better road conditions and, in many cases, took traffic away from small towns and villages. The suffering of the few people who had their land compulsorily purchased, or who found a motorway placed only a few yards from their home (e.g. alongside the Westway in London), was considered justified as it was for the good of the community as a whole.

Westway, perhaps, epitomised the whole environmental problem of motorways. However much the community wanted to travel faster – and how much faster would it make travelling anyway? – was it right that people should have to put up with the massive problems caused by such roads being as little as 10 metres from their bedrooms? Increasingly, at public inquiries questions were asked about the environmental effects of motorways, as well as the one big question – was it necessary?

Motorways had been justified by the argument that in thirty years' time the existing roads would not be able to carry the volume of traffic predicted. Challenges to the need for any major road development were based on the accuracy and relevance of these estimates.

Predictions that were habitually made on the basis that future increases in traffic would be at the same rate as that of those in the past up to a 'saturation level' of a maximum car ownership were scorned as taking no account of external influences, such as the price of oil.

More particularly, urban motorway building, it was said, by creating more road space actually generated traffic that would not have appeared otherwise, and thus traffic forecasts were to a large extent 'self-fulfilling prophecies'.

Despite embarrassing revelations that traffic forecasts were wildly high in practice (a problem that has still not been fully solved, even by including increasingly high estimates for future oil prices, and so on) there was an increasing disregard for these challenges. This led to a number of public inquiries which were dramatically disrupted as objectors to the proposed road interrupted and stopped inquiries as they refused to accept what seemed a sham of public participation. At a number of inquiries technical evidence by the Department of Transport was shown to be highly inaccurate, with such flaws as calculated traffic flows showing much larger numbers of vehicles entering a junction than leaving it – clearly impossible in reality.

This dissatisfaction culminated in three major inquiries where the Department of Transport was rebuffed. At the Archway Road inquiry in North London the government cancelled the road scheme rather than follow the Inspector's direction to publish a report on the next stage. At Water Orton in the Midlands in 1978, Inspector Hugh Gardner strongly criticised the Department of Transport's approach as 'mother knows best'. 'If the Department has a good case,' he said, 'there is everything to be said for stating it in public. If it has not, it is desirable that a better solution to the traffic problems be found.' Unfortunately his proposals have still not be taken up. A final traumatic experience at a motorway inquiry, where a farmer, Mr Bushell, took the government to court, led to a re-examination of public inquiries for highways reported in a White Paper published in 1978. Bushell eventually lost his case on appeal in the House of Lords, and this defeat, coupled with a declining expenditure in road building anyway, and some limited procedural reforms in the White Paper on highway inquiries took much of the steam out of the battle over motorways. But many of the questions remain.

In urban areas, is motorway building really going to solve any problems? As has been noted above more road space encourages more motoring and so fails to solve congestion problems. Even Los Angeles, which is built around motorways, has serious congestion and the result is a city which is up to 193 kilometres across despite having no larger population than the West Midlands.

Other problems – e.g. is the spiralling price of oil going to allow the increase in traffic that is forecast? How high a priority should be given to a marginal speeding up of a few people's inter-urban journeys? – similarly have not been faced.

A greater problem is that, having built motorways and large trunk roads the government is now faced with increasing expenditure in maintaining them. The same predictions that *over*-estimated the volume of traffic on new roads, seriously *under*-estimated the damage it would cause – in particular the damage caused by heavy lorries – and many councils are now having to spend nearly all their transport budget simply in maintaining existing roads. Motorways are especially in difficulty – as long and frequent queues testify.

We can now see that while the motorway boom of the 1960s and 1970s did solve some traffic problems, many of these problems could have been solved differently – traffic in villages could have been removed by by-passes, for example – and that many unlooked-for and unwanted side effects, such as the effect on the environment and the increase in traffic growth, were produced. Some unnecessary motorways were undoubtedly built, and remain as a testimony to the pressures from road builders and the road industry. Traffic management schemes and bus experiments, it has been said, have the merit that if they are unsuccessful they are nevertheless cheap and their traces can quickly disappear; unsuccessful roads cannot.

One of the most problematic side effects of road building has been that most unwelcome of vehicles, the juggernaut – there are more and bigger juggernaut lorries on our roads. Just as building new roads encouraged people out of cities, new roads and bigger lorries (the maximum weight for lorries went up from 24 to 32.5 tonnes in 1964 and lorry dimensions were increased up to their current maximum length of 15 metres in 1964 and 1968) attract industry out of towns.

Fewer factories and depots were needed by a firm to serve the same area. Peter Thompson, the Chief Executive of the National Freight Corporation, said that before the motorway programme 160 kilometres was considered a good day's work for a lorry driver, but that nowadays 418 kilometres is considered normal. This has increased the area served from one depot by almost seven-fold.

A classic example of this process in action is in the brewing industry. Faster roads and bigger lorries have enabled the big brewers to close down the many small breweries they inherited from constituent firms to concentrate instead on a big brewery strategically placed near a motorway – such as Courage on the M4 near Reading and Whitbread on the M1 near Luton. Taken over the whole country, and over many similar industries (baking is another example) this has meant the closure of many small firms offering local employment and the development of a few, big manufacturing centres, usually well out

of town. The other effect has been a staggering growth in the amount
of lorry traffic – and particularly of juggernauts – as all the manufactured goods now have to be transported longer distances. And as
connoisseurs of beer will know, there has been neither an improvement in the quality or variety of beers, nor has the cost gone down – a
result which is true of most industries.

Indeed, it is easy to see that over the last ten years, although the
amount of goods moved by road has dropped by about 12 per cent, the
average distance these are moved has increased by nearly 50 per cent
(from 45–63 km). The number of lorries needed to move this reduced
volume of goods has declined slightly – from 613,000–544,000 – but
this disguises the massive growth in the number of the heavier lorries,
up from 15,000–65,000 – a staggering increase, at the expense of the
more environmentally acceptable smaller lorries. Costs have also
increased with the proportion of national expenditure devoted to road
freight, which has risen from 6.2 per cent in 1966 to 6.7 per cent in
1977.

Lorries are disliked anyway by the public and it is hardly surprising
that the vast increase in their numbers has caused growing public
concern. Environmentally, big lorries are a disaster. First, they are
just too big for towns and cities, let alone the villages they pass
through. Many people, particularly the elderly, are scared of them.
And in many cases they are using roads which were designed for
nothing bigger than a horse and cart, or possibly the occasional
charabanc of the early motor age. Anybody who has stood on a narrow
pavement in a small village between a historic building and a stream of
32.5 tonne (or heavier) juggernauts moving at 48 km per hour (or
faster) cannot help being affected by them.

Lorries, too, are the major cause of high traffic noise. The maximum noise limit for lorries, at 89 dBA, allows them to be twice as noisy
as the noisiest sports car, so if you took all the lorries off the roads even
doubling the number of cars would not result in as much noise as at
present. And although pollution from a well-maintained diesel engine
is not as bad as that emitted from cars, all too often lorries' engines are
not maintained properly and emit soot and particles.

However, undoubtedly the worst problem from juggernauts is the
damage they cause to roads and buildings. Damage to roads is said to
be in proportion to the fourth power of the axle weight. So, a lorry
with a 10 tonne axle causes as much as 200,000 times more damage
than one car, or as much as all the cars using the M4 in a week. Apart

from direct hits, lorries also damage buildings through vibration, both from low frequency noise, which is airborne, and from ground borne vibration. Ground vibration damages both building foundations and sewers and gas and water mains (some of which are over 100 years old and increasingly subject to fracture from heavy traffic).

With all this evidence *against* their use it is surprising that the government is taking seriously pressure from the lorry operators and manufacturers to *increase* the weight of juggernauts. The lorry lobby is proposing that the maximum weight should increase from 32.5–44 tonnes, while keeping the maximum axle weight at its current 10 tonne limit. However, in June 1981 the government announced that it will not allow an increase in lorries to the proposed 44 tonnes, although a smaller increase, to 40 tonnes, is likely. The argument for increasing lorry weights is that if lorries could carry a bigger load then fewer lorries would be needed and the reduction in the number of lorries would reduce environmental problems and road damage, less fuel would be used too and the cost of transporting the goods would be cut. This argument is all very well, but in leaping from the specific to the general, it ignores what happens in reality. During the period since the last weight increase, when we ought to have been experiencing exactly the same benefits, the *opposite* has occurred. Costs, have risen, the number of the bigger juggernauts has soared and the fuel used has not only increased by about 40 per cent per tonne but has also increased by 8 per cent per tonne mile. In other words, things have got worse, not better. The reason for this is both the change to centralised production and distribution, as mentioned earlier, and also that the use of lorries has become increasingly inefficient. Load factors – that is the amount of capacity used – for the heaviest lorries has dropped from an average of 65 per cent in 1967 to 50 per cent in 1977.

The solution to the problem must tackle the issue from the other end, trying to reduce the number of lorries by increasing the load factor and taking the biggest juggernauts out of sensitive areas. By-passes will take lorries out of small towns and villages, but the larger the town the more the lorries need to go there to service it. The M25, which by-passes London, will remove only one vehicle in a thousand, which is barely noticeable. Larger towns and cities, therefore, should have absolute restrictions on the heaviest lorries and trans-shipment depots should be brought into operation, as happens on the Continent, where large lorries stay on the outskirts and goods are distributed in the town in smaller vehicles. This would both help to increase the efficiency of lorries and would encourage more freight onto the railways and waterways, which are often unused or under-used because of the need for trans-shipment. Put into effect, and, combined with local lorry taxation, this would help to reduce the lorry problem immediately and might also help reverse the trend towards centralised production, thus promoting more local employment.

At the beginning of this chapter it was noted that walking and cycling which constitute the bulk of short journeys (which are them-selves the majority of *all* journeys) are both important. You may find this surprising considering the official neglect they have suffered. Indeed, until recently, walking was not included in statistics unless the journey on foot was over 1 mile long, whereas an equally short car or bus trip would have been. Despite this, both walking and cycling are growing rapidly as the cost of motorised transport climbs, particu-larly in cities. The Greater London Council, for example, found 42 per cent more bikes coming into Central London in 1979 than in 1977. Counties and boroughs are now coming under increasing pressure to provide facilities for what must be the most environmentally accept-able forms of transport. In new towns, such as Stevenage, whole segregated networks of cycle and pedestrian routes can be provided from the first which are not only attractive to use, but, more par-ticularly, add immeasurably to safety. Older towns have to cope with the problem in other ways, and Bedford, Middlesbrough and Peterborough, for example, are pioneering cycle routes. One only has to look at the cycle use in the Netherlands to see the potential for both cycling and walking. Hills make many British towns a little less attractive for cycling but proper consideration for cyclists and pedes-trians alike could allow a substantial impact on saving energy, helping the environment and improving safety standards.

The environmental problems of transport are particularly pressing and contributing to solving them is surprisingly difficult for the individual. There is no equivalent to, say, saving paper or bottles. But it is possible for the individual to contribute by using buses, trains, bicycles and walking, instead of using a car. As others have noted, it is very easy to reap the benefits of using your own car, but it is very difficult to avoid the drawback of other people using theirs. Perhaps a more constructive approach is to look more closely at the activities of those concerned with transport and transport planning in your area.

You may be able to join an environmental, amenity or transport association – or start one yourself. Look out for road schemes – are they needed? and large new car parks – will they encourage too much traffic into the town centre and take patronage away from buses? What is your council's attitude to bus services? Are they giving enough revenue support? Would the money they are spending on new roads be better used to keeping existing bus services going? Are there ways in which pedestrians and cyclists can be better catered for? And lorries be kept out of sensitive areas?

The people who have most influence on the impact of transport are both central and local authorities and they can affect it now. The best way to achieve a better end is to influence them.

Further reading

A Load on Your Mind, Transport 2000, 1979. An analysis of Britain's freight and in particular the impact of the growth of road freight.

John Abbiss and Les Lumsden, *Route Causes*, NCVO and Transport 2000, 1980. A guide to participation in public transport plans – how individuals can contribute to planning public transport.

Changing Directions: Report of the Independent Commission on Transport, Coronet, 1975. Proposals for a radical alternative transport policy for Britain.

Getting Nowhere Fast, Friends of the Earth, 1977. A response to the 1976 Consultation Paper on Transport Policy advocating an emphasis on access to facilities rather than movement.

Mick Hamer and Stephen Potter, *Vital Travel Statistics*, Transport 2000 and the Open University, 1979. The basic facts of how and why people move.

Stephen Plowden, *Taming Traffic*, Andre Deutsch, 1980. A detailed appraisal of the problems towns face from traffic and how these can be solved.

Report of the Advisory Committee on Trunk Road Assessment, HMSO, 1978. How the Government decides which roads to build and the flaws in the process.

Transport Policy Tomorrow, Transport 2000, 1977. Transport 2000's approach to a national transport policy based on a better consideration of the environment, energy and personal needs.

John Wardroper, *Juggernaut*, Temple Smith, 1981. A detailed account of the way the Department of Transport and others have paved the way for more and heavier lorries in the past as well as at present.

9 Air Pollution

Philip Sharp

Introduction

It is important to keep the problem of air pollution in perspective. Modern methods can now detect and measure substances in very small quantities indeed and where, formerly, such amounts were described as 'traces' and often disregarded, it is now known that the amount of any pollutant is important but that small amounts may be only of small significance. It has been said that there is no such thing as a toxic substance, but only a toxic *concentration* of that substance. Some substances in large quantities are dangerous or even lethal, yet smaller quantities of the same substance may have medicinal use. Further, by no means all pollution is man-made: some pollutants in the air occur quite naturally, for example the emissions from a volcano. The amount of smoke that a volcano pours out is immense. Some forms of weather too can produce air pollution such as the '*Khamsin*' of the desert which creates a sandstorm, or the tornado. Pollen, too, is a form of air pollution to which more attention is now being paid, as it can be extremely irritating to some people, causing hay fever and other allergies. So, when considering air pollution, it is necessary to define carefully the type of pollution involved, and so maintain a sense of proportion.

Air pollution differs from other forms of pollution because, whether we like it or not, we have to breathe the air around us. We are not compelled to eat any particular food, nor do we have to drink water from a particular source; but we must breathe the air in our immediate environment, whether it is contaminated or not, and the body takes in about 13,638 litres, or 15.8 kilos, of air each day – some seven times the average combined weight of our daily food and drink. Most people are conscious of the importance of clean water and of food hygiene, but are often less aware of the importance of the cleanliness of the air they breathe.

Another peculiarity of air pollution is that air, whether clean or polluted, knows no boundaries. The smoke from your bonfire can blow into your neighbour's garden and house: the smoke from chimneys on one side of the street can blow into houses on the other: the pollution from industry can blow into a neighbouring residential area. Polluted air can also travel not just over the land border from one country to another, but also long distances across the sea. In recent years the Scandinavian countries have accused the United Kingdom and other European countries of 'invisible exports' of sulphur dioxide and acid rain, and investigations have shown that some pollutants do reach southern Scandinavia under certain weather conditions. But when the wind is blowing the other way, pollution is carried from the Continent to this country.

Yet another point is that it is sometimes possible for the control of one form of pollution to cause other forms of pollution. For example, flue gases from industry are often washed or 'scrubbed'. This certainly reduces air pollution, but, in the past, problems have been caused by the effluent being discharged directly to the nearest stream, so causing water pollution. Another instance is that of incineration of rubbish. Unless properly-designed incinerators and proper controls are used, air pollution will result. Care is therefore necessary when choosing controls for any form of pollution.

The causes

Turning now to man-made air pollution, about which remedial action can be taken, much is caused by the imperfect combustion of fuels used in the production of heat and energy, and the consequent emission of smoke, fumes, grit, dust, soot and – because most fuels contain some sulphur – sulphur dioxide. Oxides of nitrogen are also formed when sufficient heat is generated to cause the nitrogen in air to combine with oxygen. But there are also other forms of pollution not caused by combustion processes, such as grit and dust from quarries, mineral works, cement and lime works and the demolition of buildings.

It might be said that man first started to pollute the air when he

Figure 18 What constitutes 'pollution' is often a matter of opinion!

discovered the use of fire for heating and cooking. Wood was probably the earliest fuel and it is still used today. However, coal was certainly used in London and the provinces by the thirteenth century, and it is still used in large quantities today. It has continued to be the main fuel for domestic use for over 700 years. Bituminous, or raw coal, when not burned completely, as is the case in the old fashioned open grate, can produce smoke which consists of particles of tarry and sooty material which tend to coagulate. These particles are emitted in the visible smoke and are deposited around the neighbourhood of the chimney. Some hydrogen, methane and carbon dioxide, which normally burn and contribute to heat evolved, can also escape in the flue gases; and as we have already seen, sulphur dioxide is also emitted. In 1938, 2.75 million tonnes of smoke and 4 million tonnes of sulphur dioxide were emitted to our atmosphere.

Bituminous coal, however, can be burned smokelessly in modern furnaces, where there is sufficient oxygen and the temperature is high enough to ensure that the volatile matter in the coal is properly consumed.

During the last century, coal gas was introduced with the consequent production of coke which was found to be an ideal, domestic, smokeless fuel. Subsequently, electricity was used for lighting and heating, and later oil became popular for domestic heating on a large scale. More recently, natural gas has replaced coal gas, making a cheap, clean fuel readily available. As a result, we have been able to dispense with the dirty, smelly, old type gas works; but because of this, the supply of coke for domestic purposes has largely died out, and people have had to turn to the use of solid smokeless fuels of the more reactive type which, though clean and thermally efficient, are more expensive.

Partly as a result of these changes in fuel usage and the growth of the clean air movement, the last quarter of a century or so has seen a form of social revolution and a move away from the old-fashioned, open domestic fire. Central heating has become more popular and people have tended to use 'convenience' fuels. But despite these changes, domestic smoke from the burning of bituminous coal is still responsible for most of the smoke in our atmosphere, although by 1971 the total smoke emitted had been reduced to 0.52m tonnes, and is now about 0.40m tonnes.

The use of fuel in industry has followed a similar pattern. Wood was first used, but coal followed in the thirteenth century, and continued

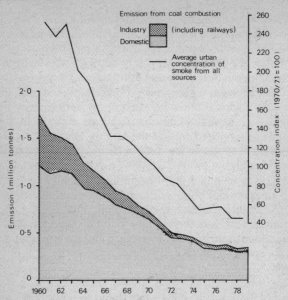

Figure 19 Smoke-trends in emissions and average urban concentrations in the UK

down the centuries. It was upon our indigenous supplies of coal that the Industrial Revolution was based. The principle of *laissez faire* ruled, and this was applied to smoke and pollution of the air. Smoke was a sign of industrial activity and a necessary evil.

Industry still uses large quantities of coal, but it is now burned in efficient, modern furnaces, and gas, oil and electricity are also used by industry in large quantities. But even before these cleaner fuels were introduced, industry came to realise that smoke was caused by the incomplete combustion of fuel, which meant that fuel was not being used economically. Soon after the First World War, industry, primarily for economic reasons, learned to burn coal more efficiently, and therefore smokelessly. As a result the amount of industrial smoke abated, but not the sulphur dioxide, which has increased as industry has developed. However, the use of the tall chimney, common now in modern power stations, helps to disperse this gas and reduce ground level concentrations, although the total amount emitted is some 5m tonnes annually.

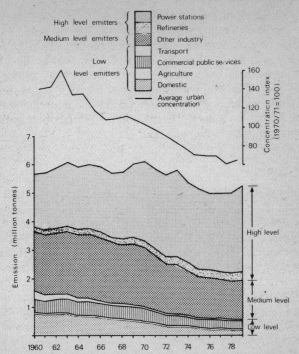

Figure 20 Sulphur dioxide trends in emissions and average urban concentrations in the UK

Industry also emits grit and dust as well as specific pollutants from particular industries, such as chemical and petro-chemical works, oil refineries and the like. Such industries are now Registered Works under the Alkali and Works Regulation Act 1906 (later incorporated under the Health and Safety at Work Act, 1974).

With the growth of industry came the increase in transport. Horse traffic on indifferent roads was replaced by the steam engine which in turn was superseded by the motor vehicle. At sea, sail has given place to the steam turbine, the diesel and gas turbine; and in the air the aeroplane has developed from struts and string to Concorde and the Jumbo Jet which have also ousted the ocean liner.

Today a mixture of fuels is used domestically. In some homes the old open fire burning bituminous coal and producing smoke and sulphur dioxide is still in use, while most modern houses are centrally heated, using a 'clean' fuel. Industry uses all the fossil fuels and electricity to provide the energy it needs. Steam has given place to electricity, and the diesel engine on the railways. On the roads, there is a continuous increase in the use of the motor car, and the diesel-engined heavy goods vehicle is challenging the train. At sea, the diesel engine, the gas turbine or nuclear power are replacing the steam turbine. All these – domestic heating, industry, transport by land, sea and air – contribute to air pollution.

The effects

In the notorious London Smog of December 1952, some 4000 people died from the effects of smoke and sulphur dioxide on their cardiac and respiratory sytems. Bronchitis used to be known as the 'English disease' and it was certainly exacerbated, if not caused, by smoke and sulphur dioxide. At one time it was thought that sulphur dioxide was the more dangerous pollutant, but it has now been shown that sulphur dioxide on its own is not lethal provided that its concentration is not very high. But when sulphur dioxide is mixed with smoke, as it used to be in London smogs, then it can be dangerous if not fatal. This has been recognised in the recent acceptance of an EEC Directive which lays down air quality standards for particulates (smoke) and sulphur dioxide in the ambient atmosphere. Fortunately, since the passing of the Clean Air Act 1956, smogs have become a thing of the past, and smoke control has done much to eliminate the smoke from our atmosphere. Similarly, ground concentrations of sulphur dioxide have been reduced, although in some places they are still too high, and indeed higher than the limits laid down in the EEC Directive.

But as the smoke has abated, so other pollutants, such as odours, have become more noticeable. Although these rarely constitute a health hazard, they are objectionable and an offence against amenity. Similarly, grit, dust and fumes are a source of annoyance and in some extreme cases can be injurious to health.

The main danger to animals is from fluorides which are emitted from some brickworks and plants smelting aluminium. Fluorides can be deposited on vegetation eaten by cattle. It then affects bones and teeth and can eventually lead to emaciation and death. The effect of air pollution on vegetation is a study in itself and more attention is now being paid to this. A small amount of sulphur dioxide in some instances can be beneficial; but too much can have just the opposite effect. Other effects are those caused by the loss of sunlight which reduces the reaction of photosynthesis and results in etiolation or the blotching and yellowing of leaves, the blocking of the stomata by deposits, and by acidification of the soil. However, as the sunlight and cleaner air have returned to London and our other big cities, so it has become possible to raise flowers where previously only privet and laurel would grow.

Air pollutants affect other materials too. Corrosion of metals is caused by sulphur dioxide, and so bridges and other steel structures require constant painting. Smoke and sulphur dioxide damage stonework, as can be seen on many of our buildings such as St Paul's Cathedral, London where black pollution has accumulated on the vertical and downward facing areas of limestone and dolomites. But the cleaning and restoration of many of our ancient buildings has now become worthwhile as a result of the cleaner atmosphere which we all enjoy. London, indeed, in the last two decades has taken on a new look after the cleaning of buildings such as the National Gallery, the Banqueting Hall in Whitehall, the Horse Guards, Buckingham Palace, and most recently Westminster Abbey.

Legislation and control

Man has been aware of air pollution for a very long time. In 1257, Queen Eleanor left Nottingham because of the smoke nuisance; and in 1273 the use of coal was prohibited in London as being 'prejudicial to health'. In 1306 a Royal Proclamation was issued prohibiting artificers from using sea coal in their furnaces, and one offender against this edict was executed. In 1578, Queen Elizabeth I 'findeth hersealfe greatly greved and annoyed with the taste and smoke of the sea-cooles'. In 1661, John Evelyn submitted his *Fumifugium, or the Smoake of London Dissipated* to Charles II.

But although it might be said that there was legislation against smoke in this country over 700 years ago, it was not until the nineteenth century that air pollution was considered seriously, when a number of select committees were appointed. Few controls were actually implemented until 1863 when the passing of the Alkali Act made real progress towards the achievement of cleaner air. This Act, passed following the recommendation of a Royal Commission, had the express purpose of controlling the emission to the air of hydrochloric acid from the first stage of the Leblanc Salt Cake process for making alkali or sodium carbonate. The Act is still in force today embodied in the Health and Safety at Work Act. It has been extended and amended over the years and instead of one process, it now covers some 3000. It has proved to be a far-sighted piece of legislation upon which all our subsequent clean air legislation has been based. It requires first that 'scheduled processes' must be registered annually, and second, as a prior condition in the case of first registration, that the process must be provided to the satisfaction of Her Majesty's Chief Alkali and Clean Air Inspector with the 'best practicable means' for preventing the escape of noxious or offensive gases to the atmosphere and for rendering such gases harmless and inoffensive. These 'BPM' must be maintained in good and efficient working order and must be operated continuously. It is important to remember that what were the best practicable means in 1863 were outmoded in 1900; and those of 1900 are not the best in 1981: BPM is a continuing process.

The Alkali Act did not legislate against smoke, but the Public Health Act, 1875, did contain a smoke abatement section, which proscribed industrial smoke as a nuisance. But there was still no legislation which dealt with smoke from domestic sources, and it was not until 1956 that action was taken against this, even though pressure had continued to mount from the early nineteenth century, when a number of select committees was appointed to enquire into nuisances from furnaces and steam engines. But whatever their findings no legislative action resulted.

During the 1880s a few smoke abatement committees were formed, but were all short-lived. Then, in 1899, the Coal Smoke Abatement Society was set up in London, and a number of other towns, particularly in the north of England, formed similar societies and appointed Smoke Inspectors. These organisations banded together to form the Smoke Abatement League of Great Britain which joined with the CSAS to form the National Smoke Abatement Society from which has grown the present National Society for Clean Air. This obviously wielded some influence for in 1913 a Smoke Abatement Bill was introduced in the House of Commons, and reached the House of Lords in 1914. It was withdrawn when a Departmental Committee was appointed to investigate the problem. The Committee's work was suspended during the First World War but was reformed in 1920 and reported a year later. However, no legislation followed.

On the domestic front, in 1935, the first completely smokeless housing estates were built, and it seems probable that, had it not been for the Second World War, smokeless zones would have then been established in many parts of the country. As it was, smokeless zones were not established until 1946 in Manchester and 1951 in Coventry. The great London Smog of December 1952 provided the catalyst. This caused the government to appoint the Beaver Committee on Air Pollution in 1953, which issued an interim report in the same year. The final report was published in 1954 and a Clean Air Bill was introduced into Parliament by Gerald Nabarro MP. This Bill was subsequently withdrawn when the government itself undertook to introduce clean air legislation which resulted in the Clean Air Act 1956.

The main functions of the Clean Air Act, the first such Act in the world, were to control smoke from industrial premises and to give power to local authorities, if they so chose, to control smoke from domestic sources as well, by the introduction of smoke control areas in which no smoke was permitted. The country was divided into 'black' and 'white' areas, although this was not specified in the Act, and it was stressed that the 'black' areas – the large cities and industrial centres of the midlands and the north – should be tackled first. In 1968 a further Clean Air Act was passed. This was a piece of enabling legislation which plugged some of the loopholes which had been left in the 1956 Act. In the early 1970s, when some of the worst areas had become comparatively clean, the 'black' and 'white' distinction was dropped and all local authorities were encouraged to complete their smoke control programmes. But it has been by no means easy; hardly a year has passed without either difficulty over supplies of smokeless fuel – we have already seen how the advent of natural gas affected the supplies of coke – or government economy measures halting progress. Despite this, and although it has taken twenty-five years, over 65 per cent of premises are now subject to smoke control. Greater London is over 90 per cent complete, and many other cities, such as Sheffield, Salford and Newcastle-upon-Tyne, are now completely smoke-controlled.

As a result, we now all enjoy cleaner air and much more sunlight in our cities. It has become worthwhile to clean buildings and to plant flowers, and birds such as swifts, house martins, woodpeckers, many kinds of warblers, tits and even peregrine falcons have returned to our cities.

Britain, as a member of the European Economic Community (EEC), is subject to Directives about the control of all forms of pollution. A recent Directive has laid down guidelines for air quality standards for particulate matter (smoke) and sulphur dioxide. These standards will be achieved by the imposition of smoke control areas in those places where the smoke levels are too great; and in those places where levels of sulphur dioxide are still too high, reduction will be effected by control of the sulphur content of fuel.

But what of those places in this country which, although they have not completed their smoke-control programmes, enjoy air quality standards which are below the levels specified by the EEC Directive? We have now reached a 'watershed' in the control of air pollution. Some people consider that we have already gone far enough, and that at a time of economic stringency, further money should not be spent on smoke control. The danger is that if smoke control is not legally imposed there is nothing to prevent reversion to the use of bituminous coal in open grates, especially when the costs of electricity and gas are already high – and still increasing.

To others it seems right to complete the task and ensure that the clock is not put back. Older people can remember what it was like before the Clean Air Act was passed, the London 'particulars', and those days in big cities when everything smelled and tasted of smoke and sulphur. But the rising generation has grown up with cleaner skies and no real conception of smog and air pollution: they must learn that vigilance is necessary if they wish to keep clean air.

Industry, too, still has problems. It is ironic, for instance, that industrial plants making solid smokeless fuel are some of the dirtiest in the country. The people who work in the plants or live near them suffer so that others may enjoy clean air. Some cement works still present problems, and some of the older coal-fired power stations are not above reproach. Here, the economic factor applies. The emissions, although unpleasant and an offence against amenity, are not in themselves dangerous to health. So how far should we go in demanding more stringent and more costly controls? To reduce the emissions by 90 per cent costs X million pounds: to reduce the next 9 per cent may cost 3 × X million pounds: and the cost of eliminating the last 1 per cent is astronomical. It has been said that the polluter should pay. But this is a dangerous philosophy because in the end it is not the industrialist who pays but the consumer, when he buys the product. The only certain way of eliminating all pollution from a really bad plant, is to close that plant down. This not only results in total loss of production, but also in unemployment. Can we afford to go to such lengths?

Road vehicles

Again, it is ironic that while we have had success with abating air pollution from static sources during the last twenty-five years, pollution from automotive sources has increased. Ships, generally, cause very little trouble. The Clean Air Acts of 1956 and 1968 applied to funnel smoke in port; and as more ships change to diesel propulsion the problem should diminish. On the railways, electric propulsion and the diesel engine have replaced the steam locomotive. Electric propulsion is clean and quiet, but the diesel locomotives sometimes emit smoke and can be noisy. But these are comparatively minor problems.

By contrast, as the number of vehicles on our roads has multiplied, so the problem of traffic fumes has become more acute. The main pollutants emitted by petrol engines are carbon monoxide, oxides of nitrogen, hydrocarbons and lead. (Similar pollutants, except for lead, are emitted from diesel engines but these are in much smaller amounts. The diesel engine is relatively clean when it is properly adjusted and run; but when it is not, it can emit unpleasant black smoke.) The emission of pollutants from road vehicles is governed in two ways. The Motor Vehicles (Construction and Use) Regulations, made under the Road Traffic Act, specify requirements for the manufacturer of vehicles and their maintenance and use, and Regulations made under the Control of Pollution Act 1974 impose requirements regarding the composition and content of fuel used. Every motor vehicle must be so constructed that no avoidable smoke or visible vapour is emitted; and it is an offence to use a vehicle which emits substances likely to cause injury to persons or damage to property.

The 'choke' or excess fuel device on a diesel-engined vehicle must be so fitted that it cannot be used while the vehicle is in motion. Diesels are subject to Regulations limiting the amount of smoke which they may emit, and for test purposes there are two standards in use, the British Standard 'curve' BS AU 141a and the EEC 'curve'. The National Society for Clean Air would prefer to see one curve only, and all vehicles within the EEC manufactured to the one standard: nor are the present EEC smoke regulations stringent enough. The smoke limits laid down in BS AU 141a were based on the judgment of half of a panel of observers, but the Society seeks a more severe limit based on acceptance by three-quarters of that panel. In spite of these short-comings, smoke from diesel vehicles has decreased in recent years, although the 1981 report of the Armitage Committee estimates that there are some 70,000 excessively smokey lorries on the roads.

By EEC Regulations, petrol-engined vehicles are required to meet standards for the emission of carbon monoxide and hydrocarbons as specified in Regulation 15 of the United Nations Economic Commission for Europe or the equivalent EEC Directive 70/220/EEC. Amendments to these Regulations have meant that new cars have been required to be built to more stringent requirements. In Europe and the UK we have not encountered the problems of photochemical smog experienced in the United States, and so it has not yet been necessary for our Regulations to be so draconian as those in America.

Lead in petrol

The most emotive subject concerned with car exhausts is lead. Although medical opinion is by no means unanimous, it is now considered that the lead emitted from petrol-engined vehicles can have an ill effect on health, especially on that of young children. When this lead is added to the amounts of that from other sources such as old water pipes, tinned foods and so on, the total burden can constitute a hazard. The emission of lead, therefore, in any form to the environment should be reduced as far as possible.

In fact, the permitted amounts of lead additives have been steadily reduced over the years, and the amount of lead emitted from car exhausts has remained fairly constant since 1971 in spite of increasing numbers of cars. Most people would now, however, like to see the lead content of petrol reduced further, even though this could mean a slight penalty in energy consumption or a waste disposal problem if lead traps are used to control the lead emissions from vehicles. The amount of lead in petrol was limited to 0.40g per litre as from 1 January, 1981 and will be further reduced to 0.15g per litre by 1985. (An EEC Directive set this first limit, but contained a clause allowing a member state to require an even lower limit but not lower than 0.15g per litre).

Conclusion

During the last twenty-five years we have gone a long way to clearing up the backlog of air pollution inherited from the Industrial Revolution. The skies are now clearer, but there are still some problems – both industrial and domestic. Probably the biggest remaining problem is that of pollution from road vehicles. The motor car as we know it, is likely to be with us for some years yet, and despite the increased cost of fuel, it seems probable that the number of vehicles will continue to increase. New cars must now be built to comply with the EEC Regulations which are steadily tightening up each year, and, it is believed that these will ensure some control. If there is evidence of a large increase in the oxides of nitrogen, which could result in photo-chemical smog, then further measures will become imperative. The problem of lead in petrol is not resolved. Evidence is conflicting, but on balance it seems that we should seek to reduce the amount of lead permitted in petrol. Smoke is still a problem from diesel vehicles; the regulations for the control of smoke could be more stringent and better enforced.

Further reading

R K Crow and J F Garner, *Clean Air – Law and Practice*, Shaw and Sons, 1976 (4th ed.). The standard work on legislation for the control of air pollution, primarily concerned with England and Wales.

Department of the Environment, 'Pollution Control in Britain: How it Works', *Pollution Paper No. 9*, HMSO, 1976. The Government's guide to existing environmental legislation and statutory controls.

Department of the Environment, *Digest of Environmental Pollution Statistics*, HMSO, 1978, 1979 and 1980 (Nos 1, 2 & 3). The source of all current statistics on air pollution.

A Gilpin, *Control of Air Pollution*, Butterworth, 1963. A textbook on the methods on controlling industrial air pollution.

National Society for Clean Air publications, *Towards Cleaner Air, Reference Book, Sulphur Dioxide, Pollution from Road Vehicles*. Helpful reference books for those requiring an introduction to the subject.

A Parker (ed.), *Industrial Air Pollution Handbook*, McGraw-Hill,

1978. A comprehensive and authoritative compendium compiled by a leading expert.

R S Scorer, *Air Pollution*, Pergamon, 1968. A readable introduction to the philosophy of air pollution control with particular reference to the important part which meterology plays.

D J Spedding, *Air Pollution*, Oxford Chemistry Series, Oxford University Press, 1974. An introduction to the chemistry of air pollution.

10 Water Resources

John Corlett

To most people, water is something which comes out of a tap when they want to drink, wash or bathe; or which falls from the sky, at inconvenient times, as rain or snow; or it is something to enjoy looking at, or fishing in, as rivers and lakes in the countryside; or it is something to bathe in or sail on at the seaside. Water is part of everyday life, and indeed it is part of life itself. We take it for granted, and when we turn on the tap we give little thought to where the water comes from – and where it goes.

All the water used in the United Kingdom comes originally from rain. The distribution of rainfall is uneven both in time and space, and in most years more rain falls in autumn and winter than in spring and summer. However, the demand for water is fairly consistent throughout the year and so some form of storage is needed to even out both immediate supply and demand, and year-to-year variations, since we can have floods in one year and drought in another. The wettest parts of the country are the north and west in the mountains of Wales, the Lake District and the Highlands of Scotland, where warm, moisture-laden winds from the Atlantic rise and cool and drop their water as rain or snow. Comparatively few people live in these wet areas, the demand for water being chiefly in the more heavily populated and industrialised regions of the midlands, south-east England and central Scotland: some method of distributing the water is, therefore, essential.

From the mid-nineteenth century until quite recently, the supply of water to the industrial north and the midlands was based on a simple principle: large reservoirs were built in the mountains to collect and

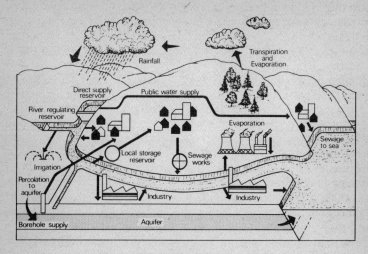

Figure 21   The hydrological cycle

store the water, and pipelines carried it by gravity to the towns. For instance, the growing industrial area of south Lancashire (centred on Manchester) was first supplied by small reservoirs in the Pennines, but as the demand for water increased these sources became insufficient, and in 1876 Manchester Corporation dammed the foot of a small lake in the Lake District to raise its level by 16 metres. In this way over the next few years the large reservoir of Thirlmere was created and 160 kilometres of pipeline took the water south. (Out of the opposition to this scheme the National Trust was born.) This water supply was adequate for about fifty years until, in 1929, and in spite of many protests, Manchester Corporation began building another dam in the Lake District! This one was 35 metres high and by the time it was completed in 1941 the valley of Mardale was flooded and the great reservoir lake of Haweswater created. During the same period Liverpool Corporation created Lake Vyrnwy in North Wales and Birmingham Corporation built a series of reservoirs in the mountains of mid-Wales. In Scotland, Glasgow obtained its water by raising the level of Loch Katrine, and Edinburgh built a series of reservoirs in the Pentland hills. These are just some of the 'direct supply' reservoirs which still provide many large cities and towns with clean upland water, needing very little treatment.

In the middle of this century, direct supply reservoirs became less popular and most modern reservoirs are now built for river regulation. In this system a reservoir in the uplands collects and stores water, but it is not connected by pipeline to a town. Instead, the water is taken to a nearby river whose flow is regulated to even out the floods and droughts. The river is used as a natural aqueduct and water is abstracted for supply lower down, as near as possible to its mouth. This system has advantages and disadvantages. From the engineer's point of view, it saves building many miles of pipeline, but it usually involves some pumping as the point of abstraction may be lower than the town where the water is needed. The water will need treatment because it will have collected some undesirable substances in its passage down the river. However, the great advantage of this system is that the river is kept much more natural throughout its length. One such regulated river is the Dee in North Wales which has two large, man-made upland reservoirs (Llyn Celyn and Llyn Brenig) and a lake (Bala) regulating its flow; the abstraction point is near the head of the estuary at Chester; it supplies water to the Merseyside area.

However, not all large towns can be supplied conveniently from upland rivers. Some towns and cities such as Oxford, Reading and London are situated on the Thames, and this river has to supply their needs. There is normally plenty of water in the Thames but it requires thorough treatment before it can be used. Other lowland rivers such as the Great Ouse are used to supply towns along their length, but one of the largest, the Trent, cannot be used because it is too polluted to be treated economically.

One way of combining the regulated rivers from the upland catchments with the lowland rivers is by inter-river transfers. One large-scale scheme which has had extensive study is the transfer of water from the lower reaches of the Severn to the upper reaches of the Thames. Thus water from the Welsh mountains could supply the city of London with a minimum amount of pipelines and pumping. Such schemes, however, must be studied very carefully from their biological and chemical aspects, as well as from an engineering point of view.

Another source of water used extensively in south-east England is groundwater. Certain rocks such as chalk, oolites and some sandstones are porous and hold large quantities of water as underground reservoirs. This water can be extracted from wells or deep boreholes, and there are many such boreholes in the London area. The water in the underground strata percolates down from the soil or enters more directly where streams disappear into fissures in the rock. The underground reservoirs are not inexhaustible and rely on natural recharging. In some cases too much water has been – and is being – taken out so the level of water in the wells is being lowered and some are drying up. Perhaps more seriously, some streams in the chalk country are drying up because the underground reservoirs which supply them are over-exploited.

Once the water reaches the outskirts of a town it is stored in a local reservoir which may hold a few days' or week's supply. These local reservoirs are often conspicuous features, lying between the older town centres and the new suburbs. They are sometimes covered and many people pass by without realising what they are. Perhaps the most famous of the city reservoirs are those in the Thames Valley which are a landmark for anyone flying from London's Heathrow Airport. Water is distributed from them by a system of trunk mains together with a branching network of smaller mains and pipes.

The supply to country towns and villages is based on the same principles. Some villages have their own small, direct supply reservoirs in the hills, some take water from the nearby rivers and others from wells or boreholes, but most now have a supply of piped water.

Two other main users of water should be mentioned. The first is the electricity generating industry, which uses large quantities for cooling. In some stations with direct cooling no water is lost, but is returned to the river or estuary at a higher temperature. In other stations the water is cooled in large cooling towers and recycled, but inevitably there is some loss of water which is often obvious as a cloud or plume above the power station. Farms, too, have always needed clean water, particularly in the dairy industry, while agriculture in the drier south-eastern England has, in recent years, used large quantities of water for the irrigation of crops. Much of this irrigation water is abstracted from local rivers and streams.

Sewage disposal

In the home, water is used for washing, bathing and flushing the lavatory, and it goes away as dirty water, and is forgotten (out of sight, out of mind). But a lot happens to this water after it joins the network of underground pipes and culverts bringing the sewage, as it then is, to a treatment works.

Industries use water in a variety of ways: water may be part of the industrial process itself – especially in the chemical industry, where it may be incorporated into the manufactured product, or used to dissolve and carry away waste chemicals as an effluent; in some industries, such as food and textiles, large quantities of water are used for washing and so gain a load of suspended solids or dissolved matter; other industries use water for cooling, and in the steel and heavy engineering industries the used water may also carry traces of metals. From the middle of the nineteenth century, many factories were built by rivers or estuaries so that their wastes could be discharged untreated. This resulted in some rivers in the midlands and the north becoming open sewers, a state from which they are only now gradually recovering. Today, increasing amounts of industrial wastes are taken via sewers to sewage works for treatment.

Some of the water used for irrigation is taken up by the growing crop, which discharges much of it back to the air in transpiration, and even more returns to the air as it evaporates from the soil surface. The water which seeps through the soil dissolves the nitrates and other fertilisers; some is taken up by plant roots and the rest may be drained into the nearest ditch or enter the underground aquifers, eventually reaching the surface again through springs or boreholes. But it is the water which is used more directly on the farm in the livestock industry which can cause the greatest problems because most of it does not go to a sewage treatment works.

Most treatment can be divided into three stages: primary, secondary and tertiary.

Primary treatment is essentially physical. Raw sewage is screened to remove rags, paper and other debris, which may be taken away completely or broken down by being chopped up finely and returned to the sewage stream. Grit and sand are removed in a small settlement tank or by passing the sewage along a constant velocity channel. The sewage is then passed slowly through large tanks in which most of the remaining solids settle as a sludge.

Secondary treatment is essentially biological, as the organic matter left after sedimentation is readily oxidised or rendered harmless by bacteria and other organisms. There are two main methods of secondary treatment. The older is biological filtration: in its simplest form, a circular concrete tank is filled with about two metres depth of gravel, slag or clinker and the sewage distributed evenly over the bed from slowly rotating arms. A film of bacteria and fungi on the surface of the gravel oxidises the polluting matter as it percolates downwards. The effluent from the filter, after settling, is comparatively clear and inoffensive. Where large volumes of sewage are to be treated to a high standard, or where land is scarce, the activated sludge method may be used. Settled sewage is aerated in tanks by compressed air or mechanical agitation in the presence of a flocculant sludge consisting of cultures of micro-organisms. For several hours the impurities undergo biological oxidation and more sludge is formed. This sludge is then allowed to settle out of the purified effluent.

Tertiary treatment is usually physical, and clarifies the effluent by further filtration, but in some cases chemicals may be used to remove nutrients such as phosphates.

The type of treatment used depends on how the effluent is to be disposed of. On coasts and estuaries primary treatment only may be used, leaving the dilution and biological treatment to be carried out in the sea. Inland sewage works discharging to rivers use both primary and secondary treatment, and the effluent is diluted and further biological action carried on in the river. Tertiary treatment is usually only used where the effluent is discharged into a small river from which water is taken for public supply downstream.

The greatest problem is the disposal of sludge, which is a thick liquid containing about 5 per cent solids. The simplest method of disposal is dumping at sea and this is practised by many large cities such as London and Glasgow which are near the coast. Manchester collects sludge from several towns in south Lancashire and takes it down the Ship Canal and out into the Irish Sea. If the dumping ground is well chosen in relation to the depth of water, tides and currents the sludge has little effect on the sea. The most useful way of disposing of the sludge is to 'de-water' it on drying beds and treat it by anaerobic digestion, during which more than one-third of the solids are converted into carbon dioxide and methane, which can be a useful fuel. The rest can be used as an agricultural fertiliser. The only snag is that sludge from industrial areas may contain too many metals for such use. In some cases sludge can also be disposed of as landfill or by incineration.

Farm animals produce larger quantities of faeces and urine than human beings. A modern family farm of 40 hectares with a dairy herd of fifty cows and a pig population of fifty sows has a potential pollution load equivalent to that of a village of 1000 inhabitants. Traditionally, the manure and slurry were used as a fertiliser direct into the land, and this still happens in predominantly livestock areas. But modern intensive husbandry, especially of pigs and poultry, produces large quantities of slurry which often cannot be disposed of on the land immediately available. Storage causes problems and there may be pollution risk to nearby streams. It is usually not practicable to connect isolated farms to the local sewage works and the best way to deal with the slurry is by a system similar to the activated sludge or anaerobic digestion processes.

Figure 22   Water authority regions

Organisation of water supplies

Who is responsible for supplying clean, drinkable water? And who is responsible for taking away the sewage, treating it and discharging the effluent so that rivers and estuaries are not polluted? In England and Wales, it is the ten regional Water Authorities. Each covers an area corresponding to the catchment areas of several rivers (see Figure 22). For example, the North West Water Authority covers the counties of Cumbria and Lancashire, Merseyside and Greater Manchester, and parts of Yorkshire, Cheshire and Derbyshire – an area of 14,445 square kilometres with a population of 6.9 million. In 1979–80 the average quantity of piped water supplied daily was 2500 million litres from 210 water treatment works, and a similar volume of effluent was treated at 672 sewage treatment works. The Authority's revenue expenditure was £207 million and capital expenditure £87 million. Most of the revenue came from domestic and industral rate charges (the average household bill was £21 for water supply and £20 for sewerage). The majority of the members of water authorities are local councillors. (In the North West Water Authority, for example, there are seven county councillors, twelve district councillors, three members appointed by the Ministry of Agriculture and Fisheries, and nine members appointed by the Secretary of State for the Environment.) The main functions of the Authorities are to supply water, to take away and treat sewage, and to maintain clean rivers. They also have important functions in relation to land drainage, coastal protection and fisheries.

In Scotland, water supply and pollution control are the responsibilities of separate authorities. On the mainland, water supply is the function of the nine regional councils and the Central Scotland Water Development Board. The regional councils are also responsible for sewage treatment. The cleanliness of the waters in their areas is the responsibility of seven River Purification Boards.

Conservation of water

Until the late 1970s, the supply of water was dictated by demand: the authorities considered that they had to supply as much water as was wanted, almost regardless of the cost in money and resources. They have forecast demands for years ahead, and have planned their new sources of supply on the assumption that the demand will be there and will have to be met. The need for more and more water has rarely been questioned, even by those people who have opposed particular reservoir schemes. Perhaps they would have questioned it more if they had had the opportunity, but public inquiries were restricted to planning considerations. However, during the 1970s there was a growing awareness among conservation and amenity societies that the resources of land and money for the supply of water were not limitless, that water can be conserved like any other substance in short supply or becoming costly, and that the demand assumptions of the water authorities should be questioned. They were encouraged in the last proposition by a statement made by a minister at the Department of the Environment who said in July 1979: 'I see in inquiries for reservoirs that the need for water is really the first pre-requisite before you get into questions as to the exact location . . . we attach great importance at inquiries to establishing the argument for need'. The inquiry into the Broad Oak reservoir scheme in Kent in the summer of 1979 was one of the first in which this question of need was discussed at length and the water authority's demand forecasts were seriously questioned in evidence by a witness on behalf of the Council for the Protection of Rural England. Eventually the Secretary of State for the Environment rejected the scheme on the advice of his Inspector, who concluded that more modest proposals could meet demands beyond those forecast by the promoters.

There are savings to be made in the use of water in the home, in the factory and by the water industry itself. One of the greatest savings would be by tracing and eliminating leaks in the water distribution system at all stages from the reservoir to the tap. Such leaks are particularly great in the older towns where mains may be over eighty years old. At the Broad Oak inquiry estimates of waste in east Kent were between 20–30 per cent. These leaks might be expensive to detect and eliminate, but not necessarily as expensive as building a new reservoir.

Over the last few decades domestic water consumption has increased as more houses have been equipped with baths and showers, automatic washing machines and dishwashers. There is considerable scope for saving water in the home, but little incentive as water (and sewage) charges are based on the rateable value of the dwelling and not on the amount of water used. There is controversy about the amount of saving that might come from metering all domestic supplies. National metering would be expensive to install, but could be introduced slowly, beginning with new homes. The conservation-minded can use showers instead of baths, and install spring-loaded taps in wash basins and sinks, and dual-flush lavatories.

Industry has more incentive to save water as the supply to most factories is metered. But usually the cost of water is low compared with other production costs, and it is only when water charges rise – or profits fall – that savings may be seen to be worthwhile. Ways of saving water include recycling within a factory, sometimes with a small treatment plant in the system. The use of fresh water for power station cooling could be reduced by siting the stations on coasts or estuaries where sea water could be used, but this may bring other problems such as long transmission lines and protests about siting in attractive areas.

One way in which resources could be conserved without necessarily using less water is for more rivers to be improved to the standard at which they could be used for public supply, thus reducing the need for more upland reservoirs. The Thames is used for public supply along its length, but one of the largest of English rivers, the Trent, is not because it is too polluted. To clean the Trent would need considerable expenditure on the improvement of the sewage works effluents and industrial effluents which are poured into the river and its tributaries. The know-how is there, but the economic climate is not right – and perhaps never will be, until there is enough public pressure to clean up the river.

It may be possible to save water, but it is not so easy to 'save' sewage. If less water is used the volume of sewage will be smaller, but it will probably be more concentrated and so will need as much treatment. Factories can reduce their quantities of waste, but inevitably there will be some, and the amount of effluent which is discharged *untreated* to rivers must be reduced. The campaign for cleaner rivers should have been helped by the Control of Pollution Act 1974, but at the end of 1980 the section dealing with water pollution was still not in force. And economic factors are responsible for the slow progress in modernising all the ancient and overloaded sewage works in our cities and towns.

If sewage is not treated to the standard which we would like, it is we as voters and ratepayers who are responsible through our elected representatives, but we must be prepared to pay for the cost of improvements. The disposal of sewage may be controversial because no one wants their own wastes to be dealt with on their doorstep.

Effluents must be disposed of somewhere, and eventually must reach the sea. Some sewage from coastal towns goes direct to the sea with little treatment, and this can cause conflict at seaside resorts which want holidaymakers, but not their waste, and which do not want to spend money disposing of it. They want clean beaches but have not always taken steps to keep them so. Now more long sea outfalls are being built so that the sewage is piped well out to sea. Most chemicals can be disposed of safely at sea, but there are hazards and some substances, such as the polychlorinated biphenyls (PCBs) which were implicated in sea bird deaths in the Irish Sea during 1969 are persistent.

Floods and droughts

Sometimes we get too much water and have floods, at other times we get too little and have droughts. Floods are natural events, and rivers and their flood plains have evolved over thousands of years in such a way that floods can now be coped with by natural drainage channels. But few of our rivers are natural because man has altered them for his own ends. The most extensive alterations have been made to drain low-lying land for agriculture. In order to get the water away quickly and so prevent the fields being flooded, the rivers have been canalised and embanked. However, the fields thus created were the old flood reservoirs, and in many places villages and towns have been built on the floodplain so that every now and again when the river bursts through or overtops the unnatural banks, property is flooded. Most houses which are flooded have simply been built in the wrong place. Those concerned with conservation may protest when drainage engineers want to canalise rivers in the name of flood prevention; they rightly protest about the loss of habitat for plants and fish and otters, but they do not always remember to protest when planners are allowed to build on the flood plains in the first place.

In contrast, long periods of drought are rare in the British Isles: and that of 1975–6 was exceptional. But this drought showed that people could safely use less water and suggested how water could be saved in the future. Householders became accustomed to pouring bath water over the garden, saving up the dishes to wash once a day, only flushing the toilet when necessary and watching that taps did not drip thus wasting their precious liquid. But the wet years since then have seen the demand for water increase; the need for conservation has been forgotten and we have reverted to our former wasteful habits. However, while people can get along with less water, farm animals cannot and they were badly hit in the drought. Many farmers wished that they had not filled in the old ponds in the corners of their fields. Now farmers are again building their own reservoirs, but it will be a long time before they are ponds teeming with a diversity of plants and animals, and probably most of them never will be.

For most of us, such a drought is remembered as being a slight inconvenience, and one that is not likely to occur again in the near future. But the lessons learnt while living through a drought should not be ignored and even in Britain with its relatively high and reliable rainfall, conservation and the wise use of water should be high on our list of priorities.

Further reading

A Brooks, *Waterways and Wetlands*, British Trust for Conservation Volunteers, 1981 (revised). A practical handbook for those managing wetland habitat.

J Dyson, *Save the Village Pond*, British Waterfowl Association and Ford Motor Company, 1974. Basic pond management guidebook.

Water Industry Review 1978, National Water Council. This describes all aspects of the work of the ten regional Water Authorities, with good maps, tables and diagrams.

E Porter, *Water Management in England and Wales*, Cambridge Geographical Series No. 10, Cambridge University Press, 1978. An independent study of the policies and workings of the regional Water Authorities.

Conservation and Land Drainage Guidelines, Water Space Amenity Commission, 1980. Guidelines for drainage and coastal defence engineers, drawn up with the help of conservation bodies. It should help conservationists to monitor what is being done.

11 Wastes and Recycling

Wendy Pettigrew

Since collecting and disposing of rubbish are major functions of local authorities, costing the ratepayer more and more every year, it is surprising that many people are not too concerned either with the amount of rubbish they generate (14 kilos per household each week in the United Kingdom) or with the fate of that rubbish once it has been taken away. 'Out of sight, out of mind' probably sums up the situation. In fact, in the United Kingdom 18 million tonnes of domestic and commercial waste are collected and disposed of annually, plus 29 million tonnes of industrial waste. Local authorities (usually the county council) will dump 90 per cent of municipal waste into landfill sites, as this is the cheapest way to get rid of our rubbish – it costs about £2 to drop a tonne of rubbish into a hole in the ground and then cover it with earth. In some cases the rubbish will be burnt, often after potentially valuable pieces of metal have been extracted for recycling. If the rubbish *is* going to be burnt, obviously it makes sense to use the heat generated by this incineration as a source of energy. Nevertheless, when you consider that it can cost £15 a tonne to burn our rubbish, the economics of such a system have yet to win favour in many areas; but the land available for rubbish dumps is finite, and many local authorities are seriously considering other ways of dealing with the waste they collect.

However, we really do need to think about the waste generated by our throw-away society, and attack the problem in a systematic way: first we need to reduce the waste at its source, and then re-use everything as much as possible. What cannot be re-used should be broken down and re-cycled in some way, and the remaining waste should be disposed of as carefully as possible. So, let's look at these aspects of our waste in that order, which is how we should be dealing with them, even though this is not necessarily what is actually happening.

Reducing waste at the source

If we produced less rubbish local authorities would have less to collect and dispose of, thus making more money available to spend on other services, such as education and welfare. This would benefit us all, although our rates would not necessarily be reduced. There are two major reasons why we produce so much rubbish today, apart from the fact that there are more of us: the goods we buy are not built to last and are discarded well before their time, and sophisticated marketing and advertising has encouraged the growth of packaging for all consumer goods – packaging which really is unnecessary and just gets thrown out into the rubbish bin.

The fact that many goods are manufactured with 'built-in obsolescence', that is having a very short lifetime so that they will have to be replaced, is something we have all come across but probably never thought about much. Take the example of the modern motor car: we spend £3–4000 on something which is only guaranteed for one year, and which we are encouraged to replace with a newer model within two years. Considering the raw materials – metal, rubber, plastics, etc. – which make up every automobile, this situation is ludicrous, to say the least. Cars today are simply not designed to last, as they are usually made out of a single shell body with steel panels that are prone to corrosion, being thinner than the panels built on to cars twenty years ago. Those people who do keep their cars for long periods of time are not helped by garage mechanics who have no interest in working on a faithful Morris Minor, and spare parts become increasingly difficult to obtain.

Clothes are another example, where shoddy work is often excused because the garment is not meant to last any longer than the current fashion which dictates that it should be worn. Even so, when you consider the expense involved in purchasing shoes is it too much to expect that they should last for more than one year? Women's tights and stockings are other items of clothing which often last no longer than the time taken to pull them out of the packet and put them on.

The situation is even worse with household appliances, as there are

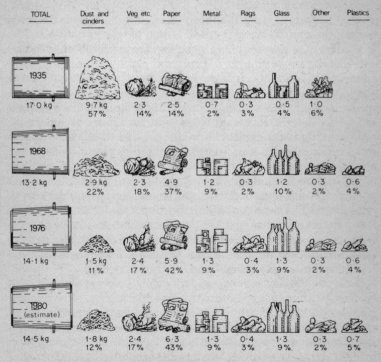

more of them in every household and it seems that the more complicated the machine, the more likely it is to break down early in its life.
One manufacturer of washing machines proudly boasts that his
machine will last up to ten years – is that all? Why should we be forced
to discard a twenty-six-year-old refrigerator in perfect working order
just because the rubber seal around the door needs replacing but the
manufacturer doesn't make one to fit such an obsolete model? Consumers should encourage the production of goods that will last
because, after all, you aren't likely to replace your toaster just because
you would like one that is a different colour or design – you will wait
until it no longer works before buying a replacement. When considering any purchase, do check that you are buying a quality item by
getting as much information as possible from the manufacturer and
sales office, and asking friends for advice. Also, do not be afraid to

Figure 23 Average weekly waste from UK households

return defective goods. Buying cheap equipment does not pay in the long run.

Of course, it can be argued that if goods were built to last longer then consumer demand would fall, thus decreasing factory output and causing unemployment. But this need not be the case – more mechanics will be needed to maintain and repair the things they once manufactured, thus creating jobs that were lost. For this reason, too, do support your local handyman when you need to have anything repaired. He may be prepared to manufacture a miniscule part to keep your lawnmower going, whereas a High Street salesman will endeavour to convince you that you should scrap it and buy the latest model. Indeed, many manufacturers don't stock spare parts deliberately, and have a policy of changing their models every two or three years, thus forcing consumers to buy the new model rather than have their existing one repaired.

When you are next in a shop of any kind, look carefully at the goods displayed there. Do we really need all that packaging, which will be thrown away as soon as we get home (or even sooner in some cases)? The increase in the amount of paper and plastic in household waste (see Fig. 23) reflects the increase in packaging over the last forty-five years. In many cases little of this is necessary, and has been produced by marketing and advertising executives to make the goods as appealing as possible to encourage sales, and sometimes to discourage shoplifting by increasing the 'size' of the item. If you think about it, do a dozen biscuits really need to sit in a crinkly pink plastic container, all wrapped up in cellophane before being put in a paper bag to be taken away? In some cases, the packaging can cost *more* than the item being packaged, which is particularly applicable when you consider aerosol cans. Because of their sophisticated design they require high grade metal for their construction, but are impossible to recycle and the fluorocarbon propellant needed to operate them may be damaging to the ozone layer in the atmosphere. Ordinary, unsophisticated hand sprays can be just as efficient – and they can be refilled!

What can *you* do about excess packaging? To begin with, you can try to limit your personal consumption of packaging, and especially try to avoid any packaging which cannot be re-used or recycled in any way. Plastics are obvious offenders here, as they will not rot down when buried with other rubbish and, apart from the ubiquitous carrier bag seen throughout Western Europe, often have no use after the goods have been unwrapped. Re-use containers wherever possible, and don't be afraid to take cans or bottles into a shop to be filled on the spot. Some shops may insist that you put your purchase, however small, into a paper bag to prove that it has been paid for. This is quite unnecessary – after all, what is the till receipt for but to act as 'proof of purchase'? Some shops supply paper bags made of recycled paper – do support them and encourage others to follow their example.

Also, think before you put anything into the rubbish bin – can it serve another useful purpose before being thrown away? Your own ingenuity and circumstances will dictate the amount of rubbish collected from your home each week, and the possibilities for re-use and recycling will be discussed later in this chapter. In the meantime, a few words about the rubbish which is *not* collected from your home,

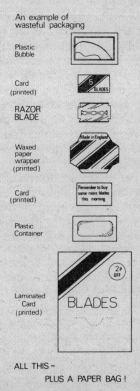

Figure 24   An example of wasteful packaging

but which you may well contribute to in some way: the litter we generate all around us.

Again, it is mainly excess packaging which contributes to increased litter, as well as take-away food outlets. At Paddington Station in London three tons of litter are collected every day – and that does *not* include the rubbish left on trains or put into rubbish bins. Unsightly litter in countryside beauty spots is deplorable, but we are all to blame as someone must have left it there. In contrast with Third World countries, where everything possible is reused and no 'litter' thrown away, the British are an untidy nation. Even legislation to stop litter has been largely incffcctivc as the fines involved are so small you are unlikely to be prosecuted even if you drop your ice cream wrapper right in front of a policeman.

The efforts of individuals, local authorities and citizen organisations to clear up litter are commendable, but merely picking up the litter is not going to solve the problem – it shouldn't be there in the first place. Several years ago a situation occurred in the United States whereby many conservation groups withdrew their support for the activities of Keep America Beautiful, a litter-clearing citizen group. The reason for this was that they discovered that Keep America Beautiful was funded primarily by the soft drink manufacturers and brewers, all of whom were keen to continue marketing their goods in packaging that was wasteful. Naturally these industries were more concerned with encouraging people to pick up the litter generated by their products than they were at supporting any legislation to curb the packaging. A similar situation exists in Britain with enormous amounts of money being given to Keep Britain Tidy by the 'excess packagers' and this brings us on to the ways in which we can encourage the re-use of containers rather than merely going around picking them up, even if they are then recycled.

Re-using containers and other goods

The success of legislation in some American states to outlaw beverage containers that cannot be returned and re-used should be encouraging other countries, including the United Kingdom, to follow suit. The reason that it is taking so long to be accepted as an environmentally-acceptable method of dealing with such packaging is that the industries involved use their money and power to lobby against it.

It is possible to wash and re-use bottles for beverages 10–20 times, thus saving on the materials and energy needed to make new bottles for every litre of liquid sold. To make a new can from recycled aluminium takes 5 per cent of the energy used when making the same can from virgin material. Therefore, it makes sense to put a deposit on all bottles and cans when selling drinks. The purchaser can then redeem the bottles (which will be re-used) and the cans (which will be recycled) and get paid for doing so. The American state of Oregon passed a 'bottle bill' in 1971, and as a result found that litter was reduced by 36–40 per cent, and although 142 jobs were lost in the canning industry in the first year, these were offset by new bottling and handling jobs. The industry opponents of such legislation argue that as well as causing unemployment and *not* reducing litter (both facts which have been proven to be untrue) it is a great inconvenience to the public to have to return bottles – and to have to pay the extra deposit in the first place, thus adding to inflationary prices. However, it is just a *deposit* – you can get your money back when you return the containers – and, after all, if you can't be bothered to take them back there are many children waiting eagerly to pick up and collect for you and add to their pocket money. (In fact, in Oregon they had to change the wording in the law to say that a 'person' could redeem a bottle or can as some retailers had refused to give deposits back to children returning beer cans as they obviously weren't the original 'consumers'.)

Here in Britain, Friends of the Earth began their conservation work campaigning against Schweppes. A mountain of empty bottles was delivered to their offices in 1971 to persuade them that deposits on bottles are necessary. The argument that the British public will not accept laws to make deposits mandatory are rather contradictory – deposits on bottles were the rule here for many years and it is only recently that the 'no deposit, no return' bottle has appeared. In New Zealand families used to pile up brown glass beer bottles for the scouts to collect several times each year; such methods of returning bottles were traditional and the rule rather than the exception. Therefore, do support and encourage the introduction of deposit-only legislation in the United Kingdom, which is likely to be proposed in 1982, and in the meantime do your bit by buying beverages in containers that you can return to be re-used.

However, bottles aren't the only things we can re-use again and again. There may be many things you can either give or sell to someone else to re-use when you no longer have any use for them.

Jumble sales, charity auctions, hospitals, schools, welfare organisations – all could benefit from re-allocation of your possessions rather
than having them thrown away in the rubbish bin. If you cannot
afford to give away anything, then do consider selling it. Local
newspaper advertisements are a good way to sell large items of
furniture and household goods, but you can also benefit from selling
off smaller items. 'Garage sales' are a Saturday afternoon institution in
the United States when a family will sell off things they no longer
need, but which someone else may be able to use. As well as being a
good way to re-use goods at a slight profit, they are also great fun and
provide an excellent opportunity to meet people in the neighbourhood. You can also sell things to second-hand shops – and buy from
them, too. These neighbourhood 'junk' shops may not be quite as
high class as antique shops, but they serve a much more important
function in society.

   In fact, whenever you re-use anything, you will find it saves you
money. After all, the 'throw-away society' we live in today is a
relatively new phenomenon and results from a new-found affluence
unknown by many before the Second World War. With money to buy
a new ball of string, why bother to keep all the odd bits left over from
parcels? Think about it, though, and the next time you see your Aunt
Alice carefully folding up the Christmas wrapping paper, don't laugh
at her, but follow her example.

Recycling what cannot be re-used

Even so, there are things you cannot re-use in their current form and
wherever possible these should be broken down and recycled for use
again. For example, although the raw materials needed to make glass
are not scarce (the sands of the Sahara are not disappearing), the
energy used to make glass from them is much greater than that needed
to make glass from cullet (used glass). The recent introduction of
bottle banks (skips with compartments for different coloured glass) in
Britain is a good way to encourage people to recycle their used glass,
and they are proving to be economically feasible for the authorities
running them. Do support your local bottle bank, and encourage
more to be set up wherever possible. However, the siting of some of
the skips is often unfortunate: there is one in Reading in an area where
you cannot park the car to unload your bottles – hardly the best way to
encourage people to bring along their empties. Again, the example of

'recycling centres' in the United States – skips placed in shopping centre car parks – could well be followed in Britain. There would be one skip for each of the major items worth recycling – aluminium, glass and paper – and often a local school or charity group would organise the whole scheme and profit from the sale of the materials.

In Britain there are many schemes organised to collect paper for recycling, although by Spring 1981 the bottom had rather fallen out of the market. This was caused by a general recession and decrease in output of goods, which meant that the demand for packaging fell by 25 per cent during the Winter and Spring of 1980–1. As 90 per cent of waste paper goes into packaging, and more newsprint was being imported (newsprint generally uses 20 per cent waste paper), it was hardly surprising that many recycled paper collections closed down. The price per tonne of waste paper was £25 during the Summer of 1980; by October of that year it had fallen to £15. However, the price for waste paper must go up again, and hopefully many organisers of collection routes will not have given up; householders and offices are quite happy to save their paper for a regular collection, but once it stops they are likely to take even longer to get back into the routine.

If there is a waste paper collection in your area, do support it and offer to help out whenever you can. If there is no such scheme, why not start one? The local authority may be able to help, and local people will be only too happy to support such a scheme if the profits will be benefitting a good cause. However, you do need to find a market for the paper, and will need a vehicle in which to collect it (a transit van can take one tonne of paper, which can be collected by half a dozen people in an evening's work). At present 8 million tonnes of paper is used in the UK every year, much of it imported. As only 25 per cent of this is recycled there is a great potential for an increase in the market for recycled paper. There is also a lot of waste paper generated in offices (particularly those with computers, the print outs from which are highly valuable for recycling) so even if you don't feel like organising a paper collection scheme perhaps you could contact a local waste paper merchant and get him to collect it on a regular basis from your place of work, school or college.

However, none of the schemes to collect paper, glass or aluminium for recycling will work if there isn't a market for the products made from the recycled waste. Again, you can do your bit to help by buying products made from recycled materials, and also by advertising the fact that you are doing so. For example, encourage the use of recycled paper for printing (it is very high quality now) and make sure 'Printed on recycled paper' appears wherever appropriate. You could also get your school or office to use recycled toilet rolls (no, not made of re-used loo paper, but new paper manufactured from waste!) and look carefully at everything you buy to see if it has been manufactured in some way from waste materials.

There are other things that can be recycled, though, such as household food waste, garden debris and the like. It all makes very good compost, and saves you having to buy chemical fertilisers for your garden. If you don't have a garden or allotment that can benefit from compost, perhaps a neighbour can make use of your waste?

In an ideal world, therefore, most of the waste which we generate would never get into our rubbish bin to be collected by the council and disposed of somehow. However, this is unlikely to happen for some time, and probably never will until technology is fully geared up to recycling on a grand scale. Local authorities are getting more interested in recycling materials from the rubbish before it is dumped or burnt, and complicated machinery is in use in several British towns to extract valuable metals which helps to finance the whole waste disposal system. South Yorkshire County Council's plant at Doncaster, for example, is proving very successful. Even so, if householders were encouraged to separate their useful rubbish from the unrecycleable stuff, such machinery would hardly be needed. It is not impossible to get people to put out bags full of cans, paper, glass, etc. so that it is all sorted when the bin man calls. (Householders in China do this, for example.) As it is, at the moment it is all collected together and then has to go through several processes (magnets, sieves, tanks of liquid, etc) to be separated again.

There is another resource waiting to be recovered from our rubbish, and that is the energy that can be generated by burning the waste that cannot be recycled in any way. A Waste Management Advisory Council report in February 1979 estimated that 6–7 million tonnes of rubbish could be burnt in Britain as fuel each year, thus saving £60 million on buying coal. In August 1979 Britain's first waste-derived fuel plant began operations in Eastbourne, converting domestic and industrial rubbish into fuel for small industrial boilers, and the potential for many more similar plants exists, although the economics in setting up the system probably are a restraining influence on many local authorities.

Another source of energy that is being investigated in some areas is that of the methane gas generated from rubbish dumps. If not properly vented this can be highly combustible, as shown by explosions which occur in dumps that have long since been used up and almost forgotten about. So it makes sense to use the trapped gas in some way; in Spring 1981 the London Brick Company started using methane to provide heat for their brick-firing kilns and other projects will soon be underway.

Figure 25 Cash from trash – the rubbish man's dream (*Bryan Reading*)

With electrical techniques being developed to extract aluminium and other metals from scrap alloys, and plants making articles from reclaimed plastics, the technology does exist to make it worthwhile to 'farm' our wastes and gain useful by-products from it all. The fact that the space available for rubbish dumps is running out will put pressure on even more local authorities to invest in machinery which can recover resources from our wastes and at the same time reduce the amount of rubbish which does have to be disposed of eventually.

Disposal – the ultimate problem

As most of Britain's rubbish is dumped in 'sanitary' landfill sites, it is worth looking at these and other places where we dispose of the rubbish which has to be thrown away somewhere.

The council rubbish dump is most likely to be a place where the rubbish is buried or laid in trenches and covered with earth. This process of 'controlled tipping' began in Britain in 1916 and was considered a revolution after the open dumps which caused the spread of disease and vermin. However, this system does take up space, which in a densely-populated country such as Britain is always at a premium. In 1979 the city of Cardiff estimated that there was seven years' life in its two dumps, but they had not found any alternative site. With ½ million tonnes of waste generated in that city every year, they obviously have to seriously consider all the options they have for dealing with the waste: finding new sites; building an incinerator; using pyrolysis or fermentation or shredding to reduce the waste; or doing nothing until new technology has been invented to solve their problems. It is interesting to note that rather different attitudes towards waste exist in other EEC countries. Many of them feel that much of the waste need not be created in the first place – it can be re-used or treated in some way. Many Continental companies have found it economical to treat their own waste, especially chemical industries like Ciba-Geigy, and even Continental dumps are better designed than British ones. Perhaps the British government needs to be encouraged to change its attitude about wastes; it wanted to disband the National Anti-Waste Programme in 1980 as being a wasteful quango, and current plans to change the regulations concerning the dumping of hazardous substances have been greeted with horror by local authorities, although the government thought it would save them money by decreasing the number of poisonous chemicals and other materials which have to be disposed of under strict guidelines. It is when you consider the subject of toxic substances that you realise the magnitude of the problems of waste disposal.

After toxic wastes were discovered on public tips in the early 1970s, the Control of Pollution Act 1974 was passed to require all local authorities to survey the waste being dumped in their area. Not all waste goes into council tips, however, and many of the real 'nasties' of the waste world are dumped in other, private, tips, often by private companies licensed to do so by the local authority. Certain wastes are 'notifiable' in that local authorities must be told about plans for their disposal and the government's planned Control of Pollution (Special Waste) Regulation 1981 would relax the stringent regulations as to what is or is not 'notifiable'. Instead we would have 'special wastes' which must contain substances listed in the regulations at concentrations which would make them either highly inflammable or dangerous to human life. Defining the level of concentration is difficult, if not impossible in many cases, and thus many poisons causing water pollution or health hazards such as cancer or birth defects will be able to be dumped without notifying the local authority, as would wastes containing low levels of persistent poisons such as mercury, cadmium or polychlorinated biphenyls.

The fact is that with dumping of toxic substances it can take many years before any effect is felt by people or the land around the dump. Even scientists and geologists cannot say for sure whether substances will still be lethal 10–20 years after being dumped, or whether they will gradually be neutralised or filtered out through rocks. The notorious scandal of the Hooker Chemical Company dumping 20,000 tons of chemical compounds into a canal in the town of Niagara Falls, New York illustrates this point: the chemicals had been dumped there decades before the residents started to suffer spontaneous abortions, birth defects, respiratory problems and cancer. The canal would glow at night because of the reactions caused by the chemicals, and some of them oozed into the basements of nearby houses. So far, New York State has had to pay $27 million in compensation to families, and still 1000 families have to be moved to escape the horror of the dump in the ironically-named Love Canal.

Here in Britain, residents in many areas are becoming concerned about what is being dumped on their doorstep. In Bampton, Devon, an old quarry is used (under licence from the county council) by a private company to dump industrial liquid waste. Residents and the town council wanted this stopped but even at a public enquiry no proof was forthcoming that the waste would endanger public health or pollute the ground water in the area, so the council had to renew the licence. This particular enquiry was an important one as it was the first to be held to question such dumping after the enactment of the Control of Pollution Act 1974, and the residents lost their case and have to put up with a tip nearby that is not even fenced properly and which takes delivery of some 7 million gallons of toxic waste each year.

It is possible to neutralise toxic substances so they can be disposed of safely without having to wait for decades for them to degrade and become innocuous. Toxicity can be reduced by oxidation or by allowing certain micro-organisms to feed on the waste, by turning them into activated charcoal, or by solidifying small amounts through incineration. Also, it is possible to reduce the amount of waste, for example by intercepting the oil which may be included in it and recycling it for another purpose.

Even so, citizens are encouraged to keep an eye out for suspect dumps in their area – dumps which may not be 'official' at all, but could be waste disposal systems of a local factory or chemical plant. People are concerned about the wastes in their area and hopefully will be successful in stopping undesirable dumping practices. In America, where the stories of toxic wastes being dumped indiscriminately are even more horrific than here in Britain, a 'Hunt the Dump' campaign is being organised by two conservation organisations to help people track down nightmare dumps. Citizens in a Massachusetts town found one such dump, and by publicising it to the local press and town council were able to force the chemical company to stop dumping wastes, which included vinyl chloride, in the area.

As well as watching out for what other people are dumping, you as an individual can help by disposing of your own wastes carefully. If you have any chemicals to get rid of, don't pour them down the drain – check with the local authority and ask about local disposal sites. Also, home car mechanics should dispose of used sump oil carefully – take it to a garage which can recycle it or to a local authority collection place if one exists. Unused medicines can be returned to a chemist to be disposed of safely.

Even if the rubbish you want to get rid of isn't going to harm anyone, do take care that you dispose of it with thought for others. Don't take your old washing machine out into the country and dump it in a stream; it is much better to contact a local scrap merchant and get him to take it away for you (and you may get some financial reward!) or ask the council to collect it. If you are in the scrap business yourself, even if in a small way, do think about the effect your scrap yard can have on others in the neighbourhood. Conceal it behind a high fence and contain it in as small an area as possible. That old car you are keeping (for its precious parts) on the front lawn may be a joyful sight to you but your neighbours may have other thoughts on the matter.

But all this waste pales in comparison with some of the industrial waste created today. Mining areas have a landscape of their own with tips towering above collieries. The Aberfan disaster in 1966 when 144 people, mainly children, were killed as a hill of sludge descended upon a village school brought international attention to the potential tragedy that can be caused by heaps of colliery waste. More recent developments to grass over mining tips and hopefully make them more stable and attractive as well as decisions to site them adequately, have helped greatly.

Oil tankers which illegally empty their ballast tanks of oily water before entering port add to the levels of oil pollution in the seas caused by the more newsworthy accidents we hear so much about these days.

On the international scene, as well as in Britain, the disposal of nuclear waste is a problem which is going to occupy scientists for many generations in the future. Spent plutonium is lethal for many thousands of years but decisions made today about its disposal may affect people for centuries to come. It is the whole question of the disposal of nuclear waste which, coupled with possibilities of accidents at power stations and the proliferation of nuclear weapons, cause many people to feel that nuclear power is something we can well do without. Everything else is the tip of the iceberg compared to the problems of the disposal of nuclear waste, which can be transported around Britain without any regulations enforcing the transporters to inform the police when they are travelling through high-risk areas – that is, towns and cities where an accident could be a disaster on a scale unprecedented by any of us today.

Apart from pressing the government and local authorities to solve problems caused by industrial wastes, there is not a great deal that individuals can do to help in this area. But we can all do a lot ourselves to control our own amount of waste, and to watch how we dispose of it all. *Your* own efforts to recycle goods and campaign against excess packing, for example, may not seem significant compared to the whole scale of the waste problem. However, if everyone did the same as you, then it would be another matter. The effect of organising a school or club 'sponsored clean-up' in your community will illustrate how people can contribute to the improvement of that immediate environment, while also showing just how much we manage to throw away today. Hopefully we will soon look upon people who re-use and recycle their possessions as being the ones who really respect their environment, and not think of them as poor or miserly creatures who cannot afford to buy something just to throw it away.

Further reading

Allen and Finmark, *How to Recycle your Rubbish*, Studio Vista, 1975.
Michael Brown, *Laying Waste: The Poisoning of America by Toxic Chemicals*, Pantheon (New York), 1980.

What on Earth are we doing at Home? Friends of the Earth (Birmingham), 1979. (A guide to the environmental impact of domestic life, which includes much sensible advice and information on all aspects of our daily routine.)

Hunt the Dump, Sierra Club, 1980. (A pamphlet with detailed information on toxic substances and guidelines to help people investigate local dump sites; available for 25p – send International Reply Coupons – from Sierra Club, 530 Bush Street, San Francisco, California 94108, USA.)

The Council for the Preservation of Rural England, Samlesbury Hall, Preston New Road, Samlesbury, Lancashire, can provide information to help citizen groups who wish to set up bottle banks.

12 Recreation in the Countryside

Christopher Hall

Most conservation is about the conservation of natural resources or of wildlife in either plant or animal form. But conservation ought also to be about the *quality* of life, and that means enabling people – millions of people – to enjoy the resources conserved. Getting the balance right between human freedom to enjoy the landscapes and flora and fauna which are protected, and the safeguarding of the resources conserved is a knotty and often emotionally charged problem. In the countryside it is complicated by the demands of agriculture which conflict sharply with both conservation and the British tradition of free and widespread access to the farmer's working land.

Factors in the problem

The three great variables of recreation and conservation are: population, mobility and leisure. In recent decades all three have increased, and mobility in particular has increased spectacularly. The upward surge in car ownership and annual holidays has been checked by the recession of the late 1970s and early 1980s, but can be expected to rise again sharply in an economic upturn. None of these three factors seems remotely likely to decline in force, although our population is increasing more slowly now than in previous years. Meanwhile the area of countryside (and for that matter of towns and cities) available for recreation is, to all intents and purposes, static. In fact it is dwindling slightly through the steady (though small) annual loss of countryside to urban uses. A much more significant decline in the amount of land available for recreation comes from more intensive farming, which has brought previously open and unfenced land under the plough or has put it behind barriers to control cattle. Thus 4,856 hectares of Exmoor moorland – one-fifth of that National Park's total – have vanished since the end of the Second World War. More insidious, because less obvious, is the loss of recreational capacity occasioned by the removal of hedgerows over much of lowland England and the eastern counties. Many public rights of way followed the lines of hedgerows and are now lost to all but the bravest and stoutest ramblers in pathless wastes of mud or crops anything up to 28 hectares in extent.

Yet visiting the countryside is the most popular form of outdoor recreation. A 1977 survey by the Countryside Commission (the official agency charged with supervision of national parks and public recreation and access to the countryside) showed that in one year 75 per cent of the population made trips to the countryside. Visiting seaside resorts and gardening were both less popular. Urban parks attracted fewer than 60 per cent, while about 35 per cent watched outdoor sport, and participation in both outdoor and indoor sport – a form of activity which attracts much greater levels of government subsidy than informal countryside recreation – attracted fewer than 20 per cent of the population.

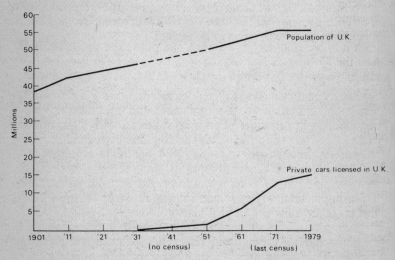

Figure 26   Increase in automobiles and people in the UK this century

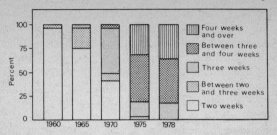

Figure 27 Annual paid holiday trends

These statistics are more suggestive than informative. 'Visiting the countryside' after all covers a multiplicity of activities. In this particular survey the phrase included drives, outings, picnics, walking, visiting the coast and cliffs, time spent at historic buildings and stately homes. But within this mish-mash of millions of people's idea of a good day out, one thing clearly emerges: the dominant popularity of unorganised enjoyment of the countryside. By far the most favoured ways of 'visiting the countryside' in this survey were drives, outings and picnics which together attracted 33 per cent, and walking which accounted for 20 per cent of the 5000 interviewed. The common characteristic of these pursuits is that they need only rural space: they do not need guides, information or interpretation centres, nor even – except minimally – facilities for refreshment.

But it is precisely the unorganised nature of these pursuits which poses the problem. When visiting a stately home or managed nature reserve, people are corralled behind ropes, directed by signs, watched over by staff, confined to a laid-out nature trail or led by wardens. But roaming freely in the countryside, they are liable to commit a whole calendar of crimes against man and nature. The clash with farmers and landowners is particularly severe and the Country Code with its ten prohibitions was devised to counter ignorant misbehaviour by townsfolk. In practice it is only a very small minority of visitors to the countryside who do misbehave, and when they do it is likely to be the result of ignorance rather than of wilful malice. In the latter case the sinners are those who would be equally likely to wreck an urban environment. Moreover, country people are not themselves guiltless. Farmers strongly and reasonably object to litter which may be dangerous to their livestock, but often themselves leave unsightly plastic fertiliser bags drifting about hedgerows.

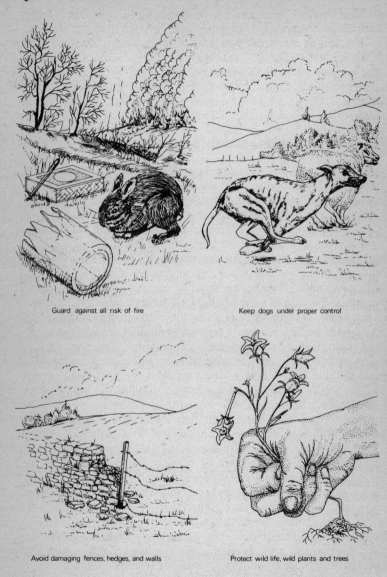

Guard against all risk of fire

Keep dogs under proper control

Avoid damaging fences, hedges, and walls

Protect wild life, wild plants and trees

Figure 28   Important aspects of the Country Code

The menace to rural conservation posed by visitors is not that of the individuals themselves but of their numbers and their vehicles.

The motor car is the lynchpin of the activities analysed in the Countryside Commission's survey which said: 'Almost two-thirds of the people owning or having use of a car visit the countryside. Less than one-third of those without cars do so.' And the fact is that cars intrude. Their shiny bodies are at visual odds with the scenery. The sense of wildness or of 'getting away from it all' which is a vital part of countryside recreation is ruined, for instance, on Dunkery Beacon, the highest point on Exmoor, by the cars congregated a short distance from the summit. The same unhappy phenomenon occurs at Ivinghoe Beacon, the northern summit of the Chilterns in Buckinghamshire. Both these sites are owned and run by the National Trust, which shows that even organisations dedicated to conservation do not always get the right balance between instant accessibility and the land entrusted to them.

The problems which the motorised visitor causes to the conservation of the countryside were entirely unforeseen when the system for protecting the finest landscapes and enabling people to enjoy them was set up in the 1940s. (See Chapter 2.) Any efforts which have been made to cope with the car invasion came later and are still inadequate. Lewis Silkin, Minister of Town and Country Planning who introduced the National Parks Act in 1949, called it an open-air charter and specified *hikers* and *cyclists* as its beneficiaries. In all the lengthy debate on the Bill there is hardly a reference to motorised recreation, for the simple reason that, at that time, there were fewer cars on Britain's roads than there had been at the outbreak of war a decade earlier.

Places for recreation

A list of all the places protected at least in part because of their recreational value is a formidable one. But as the detailed notes below indicate, designation is not always accompanied by adequate powers to achieve the object of designation or to sort out conflicts between different uses.

National Parks
Ten in England and Wales: Brecon Beacons (1344 square kilometres), Dartmoor (945 sq. km), Exmoor (686 sq. km), Lake District (2243 sq. km), Northumberland (1031 sq. km), North York Moors (1432 sq.

km), Peak District (1404 sq. km), Pembrokeshire Coast (583 sq. km), Snowdonia (2189 sq. km) and Yorkshire Dales (1761 sq. km).

National Scenic Areas (Scotland only)

These areas – concentrated on the north-west, parts of both the Inner and Outer Hebrides and of Orkney and Shetland and parts of Argyll – are subject to special planning arrangements. Applications for speci-fied types of development must be considered by the Countryside Commission for Scotland as well as by the local planning authority. If the two cannot agree on a decision the Secretary of State for Scotland has the final say.

Areas of Outstanding Natural Beauty (AONBs)

Thirty-three in England and Wales: Anglesey, Arnside and Silver-dale, Cannock Chase, Chilterns, Chichester Harbour, Cornwall, Cotswolds, Dedham Vale, East Devon, Dorset, East Hampshire, Forest of Bowland, Gower, Isles of Scilly, Isle of Wight, Kent Downs, Lincolnshire Wolds, Lleyn, Malvern Hills, Mendip Hills, Norfolk Coast, North Devon, Northumberland Coast, North Wessex Downs, Quantock Hills, Shropshire Hills, Solway Coast, South Devon, South Hampshire Coast, Suffolk Coast and Heaths, Surrey Hills, Sussex Downs, and Wye Valley.

Between them national parks and AONBs cover nearly nineteen per cent of England and Wales.

In these three designations only the National Parks have recreation as a statutory objective (see Chapter 2), but of course the protection of beautiful scenery is itself a service to recreation. In all cases – and especially with the Parks – the responsible authorities are likely to be extra-conscious of the role of the countryside as a playground.

Heading these authorities are two national agencies: the Country-side Commission (England and Wales) and the Countryside Commis-sion for Scotland. Neither of these agencies has executive powers in the way an ordinary local authority has. They cannot require that a certain development shall not take place nor cause a new footpath to be opened. They can and do supervise, advise and initiate experi-ments and projects designed to show how to reconcile agriculture and visitor pressures with protection of the landscape, but such initiatives are often taken in less favoured areas such as run-down urban fringe countryside and are not special to the parks and AONBs.

The executive authorities of the National Parks and AONBs are

essentially the county councils within whose boundaries the designated landscape lie. Eight of the ten parks are run by National Park
committees, two-thirds of whose members are appointed by the
county council (or in some cases, councils), with the other third
nominated by the Secretary of State for the Environment, or the
Secretary of State for Wales. These committees are the planning
authorities for the Parks and thus control development within them,
in the same way as the planning committee of a local authority does
(see Chapter 2). But they do not have complete financial autonomy,
and their staff are county council employees. By contrast two of the
Parks – the Peak and Lake District – are run by planning boards.
Their members are chosen in the same way, but they employ their
own staff and make a precept (i.e. a compulsory demand) on the rates
of the relevant county councils for that part of their funds not provided by the central government Exchequer. In practice about 80 per
cent of all National Park expenditure is derived from the Exchequer.

This mixed administration has been a source of dispute since its
inception. It reflects the fact that the Parks are an uneasy compromise
unsuited to British conditions. The concept of National Parks was
borrowed from the USA where they consist overwhelmingly of unin-
habited landscapes owned by the federal government. It was clearly
never practical politics to follow the same pattern in this country.
Outside of a few thousand acres in the West Highlands of Scotland,
Britain has no true wilderness – land untouched by the hand of man.
Even the remotest mountain tops, though apparently wild, are used as
sheep walks and have thus been shaped by human activity. It would
have been impossible and certainly undesirable, to evict the inhabitants of the Parks. To do so would have meant moving not only
farmers and their families, but also whole villages and towns. The
founders of the Parks originally wanted them to be run by a strong
national executive body. Failing that, they wanted them to be run by
National Park boards independent of local government. In practice
they got weak national supervisory agencies combined with park
authorities, which are basically arms of local government.

The two main disadvantages of this system have been: first, the
Parks managed by county council committees have spent less than
those which have financially independent boards. This meant that
until the mid-1970s the committee-run Parks had less than their fair
and necessary share of expenditure on information, interpretive and
warden services, all vital to the business of marrying heavy visitor

pressures to the conservation of landscape and the protection of farming. But since the 1974 re-organisation of local government the proportion of National Park costs met by central government has been sharply increased, and dependence on the local rates has thus declined, and with it reluctance by local politicians to spend money on the Parks' national objectives.

Secondly, disagreements – again usually centering on the conflict between the Parks' stated national purposes for conservation and recreation on the one hand and local needs on the other – have arisen between Park authorities and the county councils, with the Park authorities left in a relatively weak position. An example was the government's decision in the early 1970s to build a new dual carriageway road linking the industrial towns of the Cumbria coast with the M6. The road was planned to go through the northern part of the Lake District National Park. The scheme was strongly supported by the (then) Cumberland County Council which saw it as an economic life-line for its towns. It was equally strongly opposed by the Lake District National Park Board, which saw it as extremely damaging to the landscapes they were charged to protect. The two bodies appeared on opposing sides at the subsequent public inquiry. The Board (supported by the Countryside Commission) lost and the road was built – to the permanent detriment of the National Park. In cases like this the county council often puts pressure on its National Park committee or board members to put local considerations first. In turn, the Countryside Commission is pressed by government not to challenge the central government plan.

If this is an unsatisfactory way to protect what are supposed to be the most jealously guarded of our fine landscapes, the position of AONBs is a great deal worse. When ideas for National Parks were first being formulated seriously by government in the mid-1940s, it was recognised that some equally beautiful landscapes ought to be protected which were either too small in extent or too heavily populated to qualify as National Parks. (It is hard now to see why this should have been so and presumably the real reason was the continuing influence of the American concept of National Parks as very large tracts of wilderness.) Such areas became the first AONBs.

AONBs have no special administrative arrangements at all. Their planning and management remain wholly in the hands of the local authorities just as would be the case for any other piece of countryside. Statutorily they have no recreational role. The sole official purpose of designation is to mark their importance as landscape. But in fact many of the AONBs have a recreational role quite as important as the most crowded and visited national parks. The Chilterns, the Malverns and the Mendips, to take three examples, perform the same functions in relation to London, Birmingham and Bristol as, say, the Peak District does in relation to Manchester and Sheffield, i.e. they absorb tens of thousands of weekend day-trippers to the country. But whereas the Peak District, by virtue of its National Park status, receives taxpayers' money to help cope with the visitor invasion, the AONBs do not. Four-fifths of the cost of the various initiatives which have brought the Peak's management for conservation international recognition are met by the Exchequer and include landscaped car parks; a unique scheme in closing lanes in the Goyt Valley to traffic on summer weekends and replacing the slum of private cars with a handful of minibuses; a highly effective warden service to look after the Park's extensive areas of land bought or managed for access by walkers and to mediate generally between town and country; and a network of information and interpretive centres designed to promote an understanding of the scenery, history and wildlife of the Park among those who come to see it.

One of the major problems now facing conservationists concerned with countryside recreation is to ensure the wider application of the policies which have been tried and tested in the National Parks, not only to the AONBs but to the countryside as a whole. The designation of a relatively small part of the countryside for its special beauty made sense in the 1940s and 1950s. Then the planning system was largely untried, and special areas needed to have their protection reinforced. Unfortunately the National Park designation was limited to a small number of atypical areas in the north and west. These may contain the *wildest* scenery in England and Wales, but they are certainly not representative of our most beautiful landscapes or of those under the most severe pressures. Adding AONBs to the park system would produce a more representative result, but it would still not include all the most visited or most beautiful areas.

This account of National Parks and AONBs makes it clear that these designations of landscape carry with them no right of public access for recreation. What then does? There are three principal categories of free access which are wholly or partly statutory – access land, commons and public paths.

Access land

The National Parks and Access to the Countryside Act 1949 empowered county councils to purchase land for public access or to make agreements or orders to achieve the same effect. Such land may comprise uncultivated moorland, heath or downland, woodland and river banks. On land to which the right of access is given under this legislation, it is normally confined to persons on foot who automatically become trespassers if they breach any of the controlling bye-laws. These are usually designed to prevent harm to livestock, the lighting of fires and the breaking down of fences, walls and the like. Access by agreement is the most common form and involves an annual payment by the local authority to the landowner or tenant in return for which access is granted.

These provisions have had only limited use. They were devised primarily to end the bitter conflicts between ramblers and grouse moor owners which had culminated in the mass trespass on Kinder Scout in the Peak District in 1932 resulting in violence between ramblers and gamekeepers (a number of young ramblers were sent to prison). It is mainly in the Peak District that these provisions have been used. Over the country as a whole, barely 259 square kilometres of land have been opened to access in this way. Practically no use of the law has been made in the midlands and the south where many square kilometres of woods, downs and river banks which could be opened to the public remain closed.

Commons

These are like access land in that the public can wander freely on them without keeping to legally defined paths, but their origin is far more ancient and the rights conferred cover only a few of them, customary access being the rule elsewhere. In point of size, the commons are a crucial element in recreation in the countryside. They total approximately 607,050 hectares of land in England and Wales (there are none in Scotland). In character and location they vary immensely, from the huge upland commons of the Lake District and the Pennines, where common rights (mainly sheep grazing) are still an integral part of the agricultural economy, to the smaller but still extensive gorse and heather heaths of the home counties. Here common rights are largely disused, but any fine weekend sees the land in intensive use for family picnic parties, informal games of football and by walkers and riders.

It is a fallacy that commons are all open to the public. Their misleading title refers to the rights of grazing, turf-digging or firewood collecting which the inhabitants of the manor once enjoyed over those parts of the Lord of the Manor's land which were hence known as 'common land'. Thus most commons remain in private ownership and the public at large wander or play over them undisturbed only because it is not worth the owner's while to prevent such use on land which, because of the common rights, bears little economic value for him.

Just to confuse matters further there are some commons where there *is* a right of public access. These have either been bought to ensure such a right (Epping Forest owned and managed as public open space by the Corporation of the City of London is an outstanding example) or they are what are known as 'urban commons', i.e. they fell within the boundaries of a borough or urban district when such authorities existed prior to 1974. Urban districts included some extensive areas of pure countryside. Most notably many of the fells of the Lake District were within the former Lakes Urban District and are thus open to the public as of right.

At the beginning of the 1980s all commons were in the process of being registered, a process begun in 1965 and designed to clear up disputes about their status and to identify for the first time exactly what was common and what was not. The process may well continue into the next century. Meanwhile some commons have been lost because landowners have bought out the few remaining commoners before the registration is complete; and the great majority of commons urgently need a settled management policy. As long ago as the mid-1950s a Royal Commission said all such land should be open to public access, but in recent years there has been increasing hostility from farmers and landowners and from the Forestry Commission (which would like to use upland commons for commercial conifer plantations). Nature conservation interests would also be reluctant to see public access granted in some cases.

In short, the commons encapsulate the conflicts between recreation and conservation. Paradoxically, the problem of commons receives far less publicity and far less attention than, for instance, that of public footpaths – presumably because most people believe their status to be settled and secure (the fallacy of the right of access) and because very few people realise what a sizeable area of land is at stake. Finding the right solution for commons – which must surely involve guaranteed public access to all but a handful of sites of scientific importance where people would destroy the habitat – ought to be a major conservationist campaign. To hand over these agriculturally-marginal pieces of land to farming or forestry, and thus negate their long-standing tradition of public use, would contradict the principle of balancing public recreation against purely economic activities.

Public paths

There are nearly 194,000 kilometres of public paths in England and Wales (including those in urban areas). They are recorded on definitive maps maintained by county councils under the National Parks and Access to the Countryside Act. The number for Scotland is unknown because definitive maps do not extend to that country. The paths are of three kinds: footpaths, on which there is a right of passage on foot only; bridleways, right of passage on foot, horse or bicycle; and roads used as public paths (RUPPs), with rights for all traffic. The third category is now being phased out with all RUPPs being reclassified as either byways or bridleways.

Of all the statutory recreational provisions, footpaths – many of which still serve as local communications – are the most extensive, and penetrate most thoroughly into all types of countryside. The average density of paths is two miles for every square mile of countryside. But this average conceals wide local variations. In the Chilterns and in the former county of Worcestershire, for instance, the figure is more than four miles of path in every square mile, while in much of East Anglia it is barely a mile.

Most of the paths were originally local routes dating from the days when travel on foot or horseback was the normal way of getting about. Hence their status today as highways, in principle no different from metalled roads except that their use is restricted to pedestrians and riders. For this reason they give access to the working countryside in a most intimate way, passing beside hedgerows, along the banks of streams, across fields and through farmyards. For conservationists the chief problem is to defend the paths against the encroachments of agriculture. Often this taken the form of deliberate obstruction (e.g. ploughing out a path) or neglect, sometimes of attempts to close down the paths by extinguishment or diversion orders (usually the subject of public inquiry when there are objections). The National Farmers' Union and the Country Landowners' Association both campaign steadily to 'rationalise' the path network in the interests of agricultural convenience.

Through pressures like these, plus the extension of motorways and the building of new housing estates, the traditional path network suffers significant losses year by year. But there is some compensation in the creation of long distance paths, both officially by the Countryside Commission and local authorities and also unofficially by voluntary bodies such as the Ramblers' Association. Eight official, long-distance walking routes have now been established: the Pennine Way (402 km), the Cleveland Way (150 km) Offa's Dyke Path (270 km), Pembrokeshire Coast Path (269 km), South West Peninsular Coast Path (829 km), South Downs Way (129 km), North Downs Way (227 km), and the Ridgeway (137 km). Others are planned. They follow mostly existing rights of way, but in some places new paths have been legally created to help form these routes. Unofficial long distance routes, i.e. those not sponsored by the Commission, are more numerous, though generally shorter. These follow entirely existing rights of way and include such walks as the Oxfordshire Way (108 km), the Coast to Coast Walk (306 km) from St Bees in Cumbria to Robin Hood's Bay, and the Thames Walk, following the river from its source to Putney.

Besides defending existing rights of way, conservationists have a role to play in promoting and publicising new through-walks like these, and in preparing local path maps and booklets. Publicity and consequent use are the paths' best safeguards.

All three types of recreational access discussed above – access land, commons and paths – reflect the concern to provide for ramblers and youth hostellers which characterised the legislation of the 1940s and which in turn reflected the impact of the hiking boom of the 1930s. Not until 1968 did Parliament turn its attention specifically to the needs of the motorised visitor in the countryside. The Countryside Act of that year (a year earlier in Scotland) provided for the creation of country parks, of which there were, by 1981, 152 in England and Wales and twenty-two in Scotland. These parks come in all shapes and sizes from a few acres to quite extensive tracts of land. They provide for car parking and space for informal wandering or recreation. Often there is a nature trail, an information centre and lavatories and refreshments. In short, they are meant to cater for a day out in the car.

The number of country parks sounds impressive, but many of them existed before receiving official designation and funds under the legislation. There are other sites which serve the same purpose. The

Forestry Commission, for instance, is a major provider for recreation on the edge of its planted areas. Many National Trust properties and stately homes also cater predominantly for the motorised visitor. But when all these are put together they are plainly not adequate to the job: cars continue to spill over where they should not be, making a metallic fringe to the gorse and heather of the common, blocking the farmer's gateways and driven deep into the woods along the footpath. The conservationist must work to enforce the legal constraints on this kind of activity (it is for instance an offence to drive more than 13.7 metres off the metalled road along a footpath), but the effect will be marginal. More important he can work to secure adequate public transport to and around the countryside so that more people are encouraged to leave their cars at home. And finally he can press for the spending of public money to create more country parks and places where the motorist can enjoy the country without spoiling it for others. It was, and probably always will be, the old problem of finding room for too many people and their cars in too small a countryside.

Further reading

H E Bracey, *People and the Countryside*, Routledge & Kegan Paul, 1970.

Countryside Recreation Research Advisory Group, *Trends in Tourism and Recreation 1968–78*, Countryside Commission, 1980.

C E M Joad, *The Untutored Townsman's Invasion of the Countryside*, Faber and Faber, 1946. (A statement of the views which underlie the post-war planning and recreational legislation by one of the open air movement's leading propagandists.)

J Allen Patmore, *Land and Leisure*, David & Charles, 1970 (Penguin, 1972). (Although now somewhat outdated, still a useful guide to practice.)

Kim Taplin, *The English Path*, Boydell Press, 1979. (The intertwining of literature and the English Countryside.)

Leisure and the Countryside, Countryside Commission, 1979. (A free leaflet giving outline results of a survey of national leisure habits and their relation to the countryside.)

Appendix A

Careers in Conservation

A great many people would like to work full-time in a job related in some way to conservation. This is shown by the number of applications for the limited jobs advertised, and by the volume of enquiries received by conservation organisations. This interest is not entirely the result of a general shortage of jobs nationally; more and more people want to work at improving their environment, or have become disillusioned with the 'rat race' and have a longing to 'get back to the land'. The unfortunate fact is that there are very few jobs specifically involved with conservation work, and those that do exist are often poorly paid (except for government and local authority posts). Even so, opportunities do exist in many fields for jobs related to conservation: it will depend on the individual's skills, talents and interests which career is most suitable.

To begin with, students are advised to talk to their careers advisor and to do some research of their own into possible alternatives. Booklets such as *Careers in the Environment* set out very clearly the educational qualifications required for all sorts of jobs, as well as giving some idea of the sort of work that may be involved. One point should be borne in mind right from the beginning: extra-curricula experience will help a great deal when it comes to actually applying for jobs. For example, nature reserve wardens need practical experience of all kinds – recording species, putting up fences, organising volunteer work parties, taking photographs, and even repairing the Land-rover. Such experience can be gained in many ways, but active involvement with a voluntary conservation organisation will be invaluable when it comes to job interviews – and may be the deciding factor in your being appointed. If you want to get experience in practical conservation work (nature reserve management, footpath maintenance, woodland crafts, for example) you can participate in work parties organised by the British Trust for Conservation Volunteers and the many local groups it assists. If you are interested in natural history get involved with your county naturalists' trust or organisations such as the RSPB and the British Trust for Ornithology. If you are keen on political action, you should contact groups like Friends of the Earth and ask how you can help with current issues. All this experience will pay for itself later on – and in the meantime you can learn a great deal and meet lots of people who share your interests.

For information about courses, the National Association for Environmental Education publishes several curriculum guides which you will find helpful. However, a few hints as to the direction in which you should aim may be helpful. For example, the Nature Conservancy Council may favour candidates for scientific posts if they have a MSc in conservation/ecology; the Forestry Commission requires an honours degree in forestry for its officers; a degree course in estate management or land economy could lead to a job managing land for the National Trust or in a national park; a qualified landscape architect could have the opportunity to work for local government revitalising inner city areas. And that is just the beginning.

However, there are also opportunities to work in conservation without such qualifications. Computer programmers, statisticians, librarians, secretaries, journalists, photographers may all want to consider using their skills to assist with conservation work. Again, it cannot be emphasised too much that voluntary experience related to the job you are seeking may be a factor in your favour; an application simply stating 'I love wildlife and the countryside' won't help very much at all. Your interest and dedication to conservation needs to be proven in one way or another, and when it comes to working with private conservation organisations this may help you get a job where other degree-laden candidates will fail.

Sources of information on careers

Careers in the Environment: A First Guide published by the Council for Environmental Education in conjunction with CoEnCo.

Environmental Courses in Higher Education, Part 1: Universities; Part 2: Polytechnics; Part 3: Colleges and Institutes of Higher Education, published by and available from (50p each) the National

Association for Environmental Education, Publications Dept., Environmental Studies Unit, Rodbaston, Penkridge, Stafford ST19 5PH.

Careers in the Nature Conservancy Council is available from NCC offices or from the Establishments Officer, NCC, PO Box 6, Godwin House, George Street, Huntingdon, Cambridgeshire PE18 6BU. (Send a stamped addressed envelope.)

Appendix B

Organisations and Government Agencies

(Note: When writing for any information, remember always to send a stamped addressed envelope for your reply.)

Ancient Monuments & Historic Buildings Directorate
Department of the Environment, 2 Marsham Street, London SW1P 3EB

British Trust for Conservation Volunteers (BTCV)
36 St Mary's Street, Wallingford, Oxon. OX10 0EU

British Trust for Ornithology (BTO)
Beech Grove, Tring, Herts HP23 5NR

Commons, Open Spaces and Footpaths Preservation Society
25a Bell Street, Henley-on-Thames, Oxon RG9 2BA

Community Service Volunteers
237 Pentonville Road, London N1 9NJ

The Conservation Society
12a Guildford Street, Chertsey, Surrey KT16 9BQ

Council for Environmental Conservation (CoEnCo)
Zoological Gardens, Regents Park, London NW1 4RY

Council for Environmental Education
University of Reading, School of Education, London Road, Reading RG1 5AQ

Council for the Protection of Rural England (CPRE)
4 Hobart Place, London SW1W 0HY

Countryside Commission
John Dower House, Crescent Place, Cheltenham, Glos GL5 3RA

Countryside Commission for Scotland
Battleby, Redgorton, Perthshire PH1 3EW

Department of the Environment
2 Marsham Street, London SW1P 3EB

Farming & Wildlife Advisory Group (FWAG)
The Lodge, Sandy, Beds SG19 2DL

Fauna and Flora Preservation Society (FFPS)
Zoological Gardens, Regents Park, London NW1 4RY

Forestry Commission
231 Corstorphine Road, Edinburgh EH12 7AT

Friends of the Earth (FOE)
9 Poland Street, London W1V 3DG

Friends of the Earth (Birmingham)
54–57 Allison Street, Digbeth, Birmingham 5

National Society for Clean Air
136 North Street, Brighton BN1 1RG

National Trust
42 Queen Anne's Gate, London SW1H 9AS

National Trust for Scotland
5 Charlotte Street, Edinburgh EH2 4DU

Nature Conservancy Council
19–20 Belgrave Square, London SW1X 8PY

Oxfam
274 Banbury Road, Oxford OX2 7DZ

Population Concern
Margaret Pyke House, 27–35 Mortimer Street, London W1N 7RJ

The Ramblers' Association
1/5 Wandsworth Road, London SW8 2LJ

Royal Society for Nature Conservation
The Green, Nettleham, Lincoln LN2 2NR

Royal Society for the Protection of Birds (RSPB)
The Lodge, Sandy, Beds SG19 2DL

Scottish Wildlife Trust
25 Johnston Terrace, Edinburgh EH1 2NH

Town and Country Planning Association (TCPA)
17 Carlton House Terrace, London SW1Y 5AS

Transport 2000
258 Pentonville Road, London N1

Wildfowl Trust
Slimbridge, Glos GL2 7BT

World Wildlife Fund (WWF)
Panda House, 11–13 Ockford Road, Godalming, Surrey GU7

This is not a comprehensive list, but includes those organisations mentioned in the text. There are several directories giving many other organisations, and additional sources of information. One of the most useful is *The Environment: Sources of Information for Teachers* available from Department of Education & Science, Room 2/11, Elizabeth House, York Road, London SE1 7PH.

Index